WHAT PEOPLE ARE SAYING ABOUT THE
ONE ANOTHERING SERIES

"Dick Meyer's *One Anothering* series offers small groups the chance to grow together by both explanation and experience. His unique writing presents reflection on the small group process (from a skilled facilitator) and calls us to serious sharing on personal and spiritual levels. The third volume, *Creating Significant Spiritual Community*, delivers on the promise. This book really can foster spiritual community in your small group."
> —Dr. Charles Denison, Dougans and Denison, New Church
> Development Consulting

"Can another book on small groups be too much of a good thing? Absolutely not! With captivating stories and insightful biblical analysis, Meyer builds on his previous work to reveal deeper dimensions of intentional community life."
> —Rev. Ann Jahnes, St. Andrews Covenant Presbyterian Church,
> Wilmington, NC

"We have used Dick Meyer's ONE ANOTHERING books with our small groups over the last eight years and have experienced life-changing results personally and in our church."
> —Rev. Charles F. Scott and Ms. Mary Scott, Ministers-at-Large for
> Young Life, South-Central Division

"An excellent resource . . . provides life-giving experiential ways to grow within small faith communities . . . one of the most practical small group resources used in our ecumenical Institute of Small Group Development."
> —Hal Edwards, President, Christian Laity of Chicago

"If you are looking to turn your church or company into a community of caring people, I know of no better place to get started than this."
> —Lyman Coleman, President, Serendipity House

"I can't wait to put this book into the hands of every one of our small group leaders. Once again Dick Meyer has brought his marvelous experience to bear on one of our most pressing needs—growing community through small groups."
> —E. Stanley Ott, President, The Vital Church Institute

"Dick Meyer sets the playing field, outlines the game rules, and tosses hittable batting practice for small groups who want to work on their relational game. With clear, simple, accessible, and practical coaching, he guides small groups into the depth and complexity of biblical life together. With a stadium full of great stories, he helps reform rough-hewn gatherings into sparkling communal diamonds. Truly a disciple's guide to good groups."
—Gareth Icenogle, author, pastor, and adjunct professor

"A down-to-earth look at what it means to live together in spiritual community . . . if depth and vitality are what your group needs, this book is a must."
—Rev. Charlie Ayars, Clear Lake Presbyterian Church, Houston

"Inspiring, insightful, and most importantly, useful . . . Dick Meyer is the best small group facilitator I know in this country."
—Rev. Dennis Denning, Northminster Presbyterian Church, Cincinnati

One Anothering
Volume 1

Biblical

Building

Blocks

for Small Groups

Rev. Richard C. Meyer

Augsburg Books

MINNEAPOLIS

ONE ANOTHERING, VOLUME 1
Biblical Building Blocks for Small Groups

First Augsburg Books edition 2004

Large-quantity purchases or custom editions of this book are available at a discount from the publisher. For more information, contact the sales department at Augsburg Fortress, Publishers, 1-800-328-4648, or write to: Sales Director, Augsburg Fortress, Publishers, P. O. Box 1209, Minneapolis, MN 55440-1209.

Cover image: © Royalty-Free/Corbis. Cover design by Diana Running.

ISBN 0-8066-9055-0

The paper used in this publication meets the minimum requirements of American National Standard for Information Sciences—Permanence of Paper for Printed Library Materials, ANSI Z329.48-1984. ♾ ™

Printed in the U. S. A.

08   07   06   5   6   7   8   9   10

Victor Books, for quotations from COVENANT TO CARE by Louis Evans, Jr. Published by Victor Books, copyright 1989, SP Publications, Inc., Wheaton, IL.

Westminster/John Knox Press, for the following quotations:

From TO UNDERSTAND EACH OTHER by Paul Tournier. Copyright © 1967 by M.E. Bratcher. Used by permission.

From USING THE BIBLE IN GROUPS by Roberta Hestenes. Copyright © 1983 by Roberta Hestenes. Used by permission.

From THE DAILY STUDY BIBLE SERIES: "The Acts of the Apostles," "The Letters of James and Peter," and "The Gospel of John, Vol. 2" by William Barclay. Used by permission.

Word Music, for lyrics from IF THIS IS NOT THE PLACE by Ken Medema. © Copyright 1977 by Word Music (A Div. of WORD, INC.). All rights reserved. International Copyright secured. Used by permission.

Word, Incorporated, Dallas, Texas, for the following quotations:

From A DEVOTIONAL GUIDE TO JOHN by John Killinger. Copyright 1981.

From COMMUNICATOR'S COMMENTARY, Volume 8, by Maxie Dunham. Copyright 1982.

From STRAIGHT TALK TO MEN AND THEIR WIVES by James Dobson. Copyright 1980.

From COLOSSIANS SPEAKS TO THE SICKNESS OF OUR TIMES by David Hubbard. Copyright 1976.

Zondervan, for Scripture quotations from the HOLY BIBLE, NEW INTERNATIONAL VERSION. Copyright 1973, 1978, 1984 International Bible Society. Used by permission of Zondervan Bible Publishers.

*To the Saints at West Hills Presbyterian Church,
Omaha, Nebraska,
who allowed me to "test drive"
the material in this book with them
and to my wife, Trudy,
who kept after me to share these thoughts
with the wider church.*

Contents

Acknowledgments

Of course, I have not written this book alone. I am deeply indebted to my wife, Trudy, who has encouraged me to write it for the past five years. I also thank her for helping proofread the text and for her constructive criticisms. Then there were Marna Davidson, Sue Smith, and Pat Minard, who corrected the grammar and made insightful comments and suggestions for additions to the book; and Diane Handley, who organized so much of the correspondence related to this book.

This book would not have been possible without the support of the Faith at Work community, and I am grateful for this network of people across the country who have given me nourishment and encouragement.

Last, but not least, I want to thank the "groupies" at West Hills Presbyterian Church in Omaha, Nebraska, who "test drove" these exercises for eight years, working out the "bugs" before this material appeared here in its final form.

Introduction

My stepfather worked as a "quality control inspector" for most of his life. His task was to inspect thermostats before they were shipped from the South Pasadena factory where he worked. As his job title indicated, this was done to ensure the quality of his company's product.

In a sense, that is the purpose of this book — to ensure the quality of small group life in the church. Let me rephrase that — the purpose of this book is to *improve* the quality of small group life in the church. No one can guarantee the success of any small group. There are too many variables, not the least of which is that we all continue falling short of God's glory.

When people gather there will be problems. Even our Lord's small group had its ups and downs. They experienced a breakdown in confidentiality with Judas, and they squabbled among themselves — like the time they became angry with James and John for asking Jesus for the seats of honor next to him in the Kingdom (Mark 10:35–45).

There is no such thing as a perfect small group. Each has room to grow. Instead there are healthy and sick groups, exciting and dull groups; and I hope this book will help improve the quality of life in yours, whether you consider it healthy, sick, or just needing a shot in the arm.

In this attempt we will venture "back to the basics," to "one another" passages in Scripture. You might recall that passages like "love one another," "pray for one another," and "bear one another's burdens" were given as directives to the church concerning its life together. As the basic building blocks of Christian fellowship, they characterize the ways we should relate to one another within the Body of Christ.

To see how your small group is doing, the studies and exercises in this book concentrate on "one another" passages that I feel are most critical to a healthy, meaningful small group. The eight I have chosen are:

"Love one another" (John 13:34)
"Pray for one another" (James 5:16)
"Care for one another" (I Corinthians 12:24b–25)
"Bear one another's burdens" (Galatians 6:2)
"Encourage and build up one another" (I Thessalonians 5:11)
"Submit to one another" (Ephesians 5:21)
"Admonish one another" (Colossians 3:16)
"Spur one another toward love and good deeds"
    (Hebrews 10:24)

You might want to use these studies as a "starter series" for a new small group to help it begin on the right foot. After fourteen years overseeing small group life in two congregations, I have seen groups succeed and fail for numerous reasons. One glaring cause is deficient "quality control." When begun without adequate direction, a group may flounder and fail unnecessarily. Even though we cannot ensure its success, we can introduce positive factors to help launch a new group and make a negative experience less likely.

You might want to use these studies as a "refresher course" for already existing groups. Groups in our congregation, some of which have been together for years, have remarked how the "one another" passages have helped re-focus their group to function in a healthier, more positive manner.

Each chapter includes a study for the group, a format to follow, and tips for small group life. However, feel free to adapt the format to your group.

Some groups might benefit more from completing the chapter exercises before doing the assigned reading. Others may be better served by following the suggested format — that is, reading a chapter prior to meetings, then doing exercises when the group meets. Choose what is best for you and, above all, have fun with the exercises — to help your group become all it can be.

Preparation

The material in this book is best suited for groups ranging from three to twelve people. If you are not currently in a small group, consider asking some friends and acquaintances to join with you in such an adventure or put an announcement in your church bulletin about the formation of a new small group, complete with a phone number and a contact person who can answer questions about the group.

As you inform people about the group, tell them where it will meet. Homes are the warmest and coziest. Also, tell people you would like them to make an initial three month commitment to the group. If the group meets weekly, for two hours at a time, this will enable you to complete the eleven sessions in this book. If the group decides to meet every other week, at least you will be able to complete half of the studies contained here. Generally speaking, the more often the group meets (weekly versus bi-weekly versus monthly), the deeper the relationships will become. Furthermore, by asking for a three month commitment and not leaving it open-ended, you are providing individuals with a graceful exit point in case the group is not to their liking. After everyone is on board, tell them to *read the Introduction and the first chapter of this book before the first meeting*.

In addition, before the first meeting, do the following:

● *Consider the room where you will meet.*

Is it well lighted? Temperature comfortable? Chairs arranged so everyone can easily see and talk with one another?

Try arranging chairs in a circle and avoid seating three people on a couch. We relate most easily and freely to others when we have good eye contact. This is difficult for people on either end of a sofa if someone is seated between them. Try having people sit at the same physical height and avoid seating anyone behind someone else.

● *Discuss who will facilitate your meetings.*

This is not an authority or "answer person." Rather, the facilitator (or enabler) guides the group through the agenda, models answers to the study questions, watches the time, and makes sure everyone has a chance to participate. The enabler has an important role in helping to create an atmosphere of openness and inclusiveness.

It usually works best to choose one or two people in advance who will enable the study. Some groups may pass the leadership from one member to another in turns. Decide informally before you meet how enabling will be handled.

CHAPTER 1

Fellowship with One Another

*They devoted themselves
to the apostles' teaching
and to the fellowship,
to the breaking of the bread
and to prayer.*

Acts 2:42 (NIV)

S o you decided to join a small group! What contributed to your decision? Did you give it much forethought? Were you dragged into the group kicking and screaming, or did you come willingly and expectantly? How are you feeling now about your decision?

If this is a new group, you probably are feeling a little nervous. On the one hand, you really do want to know these people and have them know you. Yet, you are somewhat hesitant. You wonder, "What will they be like?" You ask yourself, "Will they accept me? Will they expect too much of me? What happens if we cannot agree on things? What if they see things differently? What if they are too religious? How will I get out of this group if I do not like it?"

If this is an ongoing group, maybe you are over your initial nervousness, but I ask again: Why did you decide to join a small group? Do you remember your reasons? Have they changed over the weeks, months, or years of your meeting together? Why are you still a part of it?

I have participated in small group life for the past seventeen years. Some groups have been terrific. Others, I would just as soon forget. But I am still committed to small group life because:

1) Small groups are biblical.

One of Jesus' first acts when he began his public ministry was to form a small group. In Mark's gospel we read, "He appointed twelve — designating them apostles — that they might be with him and that he might send them out to preach and to have authority to drive out demons" (Mark 3:14–15, NIV).

Jesus carried out his public ministry in the context of that small group. He spent three years with them in close fellowship. He asked them to join the group because he wanted their support and encouragement, he wanted to team with them in ministry. And he also wanted to establish a model for generations to come as the context in which we are to live out our journey of faith. Future generations would remember what Jesus had done, how he had called together his twelve, so we too would call together our twelve.

Thankfully, the early church followed Jesus' example. The saints gathered regularly in their homes for small group fellowship (Acts 2:42). Moreover, the Apostle John stressed group fellowship to those close to him. Writing to churches in the Asian province (modern Turkey) he reminded them, "If we walk in the light, as He is in the light, then we have fellowship with one another" (I John 1:7, RSV).

The Greek word John used for fellowship, "koinonia," is very interesting, referring as it does to a most intimate sort of association. Ed Bauman, a Methodist clergyperson, defines the word as "life-sharing."[1] Thus, koinonia means much more than a kind of social interaction occurring at many fellowship halls or at church potluck suppers. Koinonia is the sort of in-depth camaraderie Jesus shared with his disciples.

So, when it came to small group life, Jesus modeled it, the early church practiced it, and the Apostle John proclaimed it.

*2) Small groups allow me to rub shoulders with people
of differing views.*

I need those with whom I disagree to overcome "tunnel vision." I need to be challenged, stretched, and called upon to think through my parochial views of the world. A small group helps me do that.

In my small group I think of Hank, whose died-in-the-wool Republicanism differs from my Democratic Party leanings. Then there is Marna, whose biblical feminism makes me think about women and ministry in new ways. Marshall and Mona are a generation older than my wife, Trudy, and I. They help our group see what it is like to be parents of grown children. Without them, I would be even blinder to what my parents went through with me. Furthermore, as Marshall and Mona share their joys and sorrows over their children, they heighten my understanding and appreciation for my own parents.

3) A small group gives me a place to talk about spiritual things.

I can talk about the economy and my beloved UCLA Bruins in many places. But there are very few places where I feel free to talk about spiritual things. People in a small group provide the atmosphere and opportunity for such dialogue. They do not change the subject when I mention God.

A special place to share spiritual matters is especially helpful in my relationship with Trudy. It is not always easy to reach such a deep spiritual level. We seem quite able to talk easily about everything *but* spiritual matters. The cause may sometimes be time constraints, at other times it may be the fear of sharing such intimacy. A weekly small group provides a regular refuge (an oasis) in which we can share our spiritual experiences. I thank God for the small group that allows us to comfortably share our spiritual journeys and prayer concerns.

4) A small group helps me to experience the power of prayer.

A favorite moment for me in a small group is listening to others answer the question, "How can we be with you in prayer this coming week?" The reason? It is a prelude to power.

Through the years, members of my small group and I have witnessed terrific answers to our prayers. We would not have experienced them if we had not been asking for prayer and *then* listening for God's response. The process of asking prepares us for receiving. As we ask, we begin looking for God to work. Without praying for specific people and situations, like Lynn's difficult pregnancy and Marshall's business ventures, we would not have waited so expectantly. As a result, we would have missed much of God's daily working in our lives. The weekly discipline of sharing prayer concerns and praying for one another keeps me in touch with the power of prayer and the power, mercy, and wisdom of God.

*5) A small group provides me with much needed
support and encouragement.*

As Jesus needed a handful of people "with him," so do I.

This is especially true at two times — when I fail and when I dream. Our world can be tough on failures, and our dreams can be very fragile. In the midst of our failures and dreams, we need much nurturing and encouraging.

An incident from author Dr. Alan Loy McGinnis' life comes to mind. At one time, back in my seminary days, Loy and I teamed together in ministry. He was the Senior Pastor, and I worked with Junior High students at the church. Since then, I have become a Senior Pastor myself, and Loy left pastoral ministry to counsel, write, and lead motivational conferences. He tells this personal story of support and encouragement:

> I was once waiting to speak at a sales conference, when the year's awards were being given to the outstanding salespeople. One woman, who had performed spectacularly that year and who had made an extraordinary amount of money, gave all the credit to her sales manager. As she stood before the crowd of 3,000 people, clutching the award for best producer of the year, she recalled the slump she had been in two years previously. The future had looked so bleak that she was ready to resign and had even called her supervisor several times to quit. But the manager kept persuading her that she had not tried long enough, that she would not have been hired if there had not been unusual potential in her. Her voice cracked as she related the story. Then she made this insightful remark: "For all those months when I wanted to quit and didn't think I had any future, Joan believed in me more than I believed in myself. She wanted me to succeed more than I did."[2]

There are a dozen Joans in my small group, and they have encouraged me to do more than I ever thought possible.

6) A small group keeps me accountable.

At times I need a cheerleader. At other times I need a kick in the pants or someone to keep my feet to the fire. A small group does this for me.

I do not always remember to do what I say I will. At those times it is helpful when the group gathers the next week and says, "Well, Dick, how did your talk with your son go?" Or, "How many times did you have your quiet time last week?" It is good (most of the time!) to know people are going to take me at my word and check up on me the following week.

If they did not keep me accountable, I would let a lot slide. Knowing I need to report in the next week keeps me on my toes. It also causes me to think seriously about how I want the group to pray for me. Unless I am serious about doing something, I had better not share it with my group. If I am not serious, they will remind me of my intention and ask if I really mean to do it. They can be tough, but they are so necessary to my spiritual growth.

The Small Group Experience

These, then, are the reasons I am committed to small group life. I also am committed to making it a positive experience for as many people as possible, because of two personal and very early small group experiences.

I was introduced to small group life in the fall of 1971. A requirement of Dr. Bob Munger's course on evangelism at Fuller Theological Seminary was to participate in a small group of four. I did not know it at the time, but at the seminary he required this of students in all his courses, even those in his church administration course!

It was my first year of seminary. I was new to Christianity and was wondering if I really belonged in the seminary. Had it been a good decision to leave my job with the Boise YMCA to do this? Had God really called me to professional ministry, or was it brought about by something I ate one night?

Even though I initially grumbled about having to do something so "worthless" as joining a small group of strangers, just to pass Munger's class, they did something wonderful in my life. As I got to know them, I realized that other seminarians in the group had similar questions and doubts. They, too, wrestled with their call to ministry and wondered if they could cut it at seminary. I was not alone. I experienced a sense of belonging.

That was my early, positive experience. Almost concurrently, however, I had a negative small group experience. It took place in the church I was serving during my seminary years. The leader of the group was into "encounter " and "sensitivity" fads, and the group was a disaster. There was little structure, and it was very confrontational. I felt I had to share more of myself than I wanted to, and the group disbanded in six weeks. (It seemed like six years.)

I began pondering the difference between the two groups — reflecting on why one was so good and the other so bad — while looking for elements that contributed to healthy small groups, elements that facilitated, rather than blocked, koinonia. I took courses on small group dynamics and attended conferences and workshops, reading as much as I could on small group life.[3]

My reading and study led me back to the "one another" passages in the Bible. What the experts were saying about building blocks for healthy small groups was right there in Scripture. Phrases like "love one another," "bear one another's burdens," and "pray for one another" captured the essence of the counsel for healthy and growing groups.

In the chapters that follow, we will look at some of these passages, reflect on their meaning and implications, and suggest ways to incorporate them into your group, whether new or well-established.

The Importance of "History-Giving"

To prepare for small group study, begin by sharing your history with one another. There are two reasons:

First, when we share our history, we are in good company: The Almighty (especially in the Old Testament) does the very same thing! For example, in Joshua, God describes the nature of Deity not in metaphysical terms but rather in a personal, historical way. God said, "I took your father Abraham from the land beyond the River and led him throughout Canaan, and gave him many descendants" (Josh. 24:3, NIV), and the Creator continues in this same vein for the next twelve verses.

God continues to be self-revealing in and through history, especially in the person of Jesus, who is God's revelation par excellence.

The second reason we share our history is that it enables people to love us. I think of Jeff. The first night of our new small group he sat with arms folded, the frown on his face nonverbally communicating, "I dare you to get close to me." His presence hardly contributed to the members' comfort level, including mine! In fact, some members afterward confided and wondered to me if they wanted him in the group. Yet, because we had signed a ten-week covenant, we persevered in the hope of learning something, however painful, from our experience with Jeff.

During the next few weeks, something happened that changed Jeff and our feelings toward him. As we shared past events and memories, we learned why he kept people away. We heard about his painful childhood with a stern father, who disciplined forcefully but affirmed infrequently. Jeff was raised in a rural area ten miles away from his nearest neighbor, and in his isolation he missed learning some important relational skills. Added to this, Jeff's marriage had ended in divorce, and he felt rejected by the one person with whom he had risked sharing himself.

We began to understand why Jeff had so much trouble allowing people into his life. His gruff, antagonistic manner was a defense against being hurt again. He had signed up for the small group because he desperately wanted to be loved and to learn how to love others.

Knowing about his painful and broken past helped us to understand and accept his sometimes gruff and closed exterior. The same applies elsewhere. If the group knows someone comes from an expressive, demonstrative family, they will understand why that person may more freely share his or her feelings. If the group knows someone has lost a child, they will better understand that person's mood changes around Mother's or Father's Day. Knowing the life events that have marked individuals helps us tailor our care for them.

That is why it is important to share some history with one another. It is also a good way to begin a small group. Telling some stories from our past is a relatively nonthreatening way of warming up to and getting to know one another. So for your first study, work through the following small group exercise.

STUDY ONE
Getting to Know One Another

1. **Welcome** (*10–15 minutes*)
The facilitator welcomes everyone and asks each member to take turns answering this three-part question:

- Where were you raised?
- What was that place's claim to fame?
- What color would describe your day?

The leader begins by saying something like, "I was raised in Glendale, California, and that city's claim to fame was John Wayne attending Glendale High School. The color that describes my day is yellow because ..."

After the leader shares, go clockwise around the circle, giving each member a turn but allowing anyone freedom to pass. No one should feel pressured to answer or share when they are not ready or willing.

2. **History-Giving Shield** (*30–45 minutes*)
Significant events help make you the person you are today. Divide your life into thirds. For example, if you are forty-five years old, the first third of your life would be age 0–15, the second third 16–30, and the final third 31–45. In the shield below, draw or symbolize a significant event from your life in each time period. In

the section labeled "NOW," symbolize what you hope to receive from this group. After you have finished, share your shield with the other members.

MY SHIELD

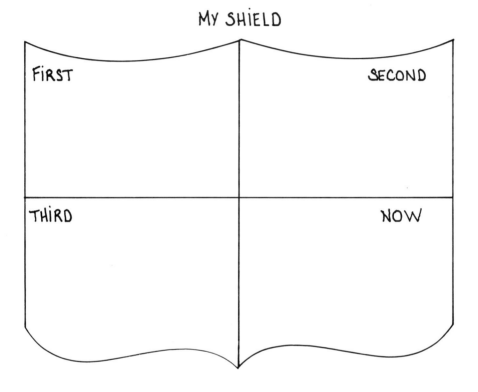

3. **Discussion** *(15 minutes)*
The facilitator asks for comments or clarification of the assigned reading material. What stood out? What grabbed you? What needs further clarification?

4. **Group Covenant** *(15 minutes)*
Go over the minimum requirements listed below for the group. Add any others the group feels are necessary. Discuss and agree to at least the following three:

a. Make group meeting a top priority, missing only when ill or out of town.
b. Come willing to fully participate, preparing for each meeting, being open to God's presence and to others in the group.
c. Be willing to respect the confidence of each group member. What is shared in the group stays in the group.
d. Give each other permission to pass. If any member feels uncomfortable sharing, he/she may simply say, "I pass." The group will respect the person's privacy.

5. **Prayer Concerns** *(15–25 minutes)*

As time allows, share how members might pray for you this coming week. The facilitator begins the sharing and keeps track of the time remaining.

6. **Prayer** *(5 minutes)*

Close in silent prayer, taking two or three minutes of silence to thank God for what you have learned about yourself and one another. Also pray in silence for any needs mentioned.

7. **Assignment**

Assign Chapter 2 for next week's reading.

CHAPTER 2

Love
One
Another

A new commandment I give to you,
that you love one another,
even as I have loved you,
that you also love one another.

John 13:34 (RSV)

On November 8, 1981, Will Durant died. Durant was a highly respected scholar, historian, and philosopher. He and his wife, Ariel, wrote a monumental work entitled *The History of Civilization*; and just before his death, at age 92, he was interviewed on television. (Given my interest in history, I watched the interview with great fascination and was not disappointed.) Reflecting on a lifetime of studying and writing about people and events, Durant said, "My final lesson of history is the same as that of Jesus." He continued, with a chuckle, "You may think it is a lollipop but just try it — love one another."[1]

One could write an entire book on the importance of love in the Old and New Testaments. In fact, I just finished reading one entitled *Testaments of Love: A Study of Love in the Bible*, by Leon Morris.[2] The book is 298 pages long with fine print, footnotes, and no pictures!

Herein lurks our challenge. It comes as no surprise that a central building block of the church and of a healthy small group is love. Even those outside the church know love was central to Jesus and to those who have followed him through the centuries. The challenge, then, given the immensity of this topic, is where does one begin in talking about love?

One of the best places to begin is John's gospel. In the thirteenth chapter we catch a glimpse of what Jesus meant by his call to love. What Jesus says may surprise us, however, because the radical kind of loving to which he calls us rarely is found in the church today.

Before reading the text, here is a reminder of the scene. Jesus' words were his opening lines in his farewell address to his disciples. They have gathered in the Upper Room. They have shared much over the past three years. They have laughed together, loved and cried together. Now the remaining time is short. Judas has just left to betray Jesus. With him gone, Jesus turns to his disciples and says:

> My children, I will be with you only a little
> longer. You will look for me, and just as I told the

Jews, so I tell you now: Where I am going, you
cannot come.

A new command I give you: Love one another.
As I have loved you, so you must love one another.
By this all men will know that you are my disciples,
if you love one another. (John 13:33-35, NIV)

A New Way?

Upon reading Jesus' words one wonders what he meant by
love being a "new" command. After all, love itself is not a new
commandment but an old one. We find it recorded in the Levitical
Law — "Love your neighbor as yourself" (Lev. 19:18, NIV).

Since this commandment had been around for centuries,
why would Jesus call it "new"? As a child had he fallen asleep
when those verses were covered in Sabbath School? Hardly. A
couple of other possibilities make more sense. For example, some
say the reason for the "newness" of the commandment had to do
with it being a specific command to the church, rather than a
universal command. In other words, Jesus is not speaking of love
to be shared with people everywhere, but rather to be shared
within the fellowship of Christ.

This may be true, but I prefer another possibility. John
Killinger, in his work *A Devotional Guide to John*, states, "The 'newness' of the commandment lay not in the commandment itself
but in the motivational clause attached to it: Love one another *as
I have loved you.*"[3]

A new, deeper dimension has been added. The example is
Christ. We are called to love one another as Jesus loved his disciples. Therefore, to become the kind of loving community Christ
modeled, we must pay close attention to how he loved his disciples. For, as he loved them, we are to love one another in the
church.

How did Jesus love his disciples? What characterized his
love for them? William Barclay, in his commentary on John from
the *The Daily Study Bible Series*,[4] suggests that Jesus loved his disciples in four ways: selflessly, sacrificially, understandingly, and

forgivingly. I suggest three additional essentials of Christ-like love: realistically, intimately, and intentionally.

Essentials of Love

First, Jesus loved the disciples *realistically.* That is, he set limits around his loving. One of the greatest lessons he taught his disciples was that it is impossible to love everyone with the same intensity and commitment. Loving takes time. As Dr. Alan Loy McGinnis stated, "Loving relationships are built up over the years, like a fine lacquer finish, with the accumulated layers of many acts of kindness."[5]

Unfortunately, there are not enough hours in the day to love everyone in this way. The disciples saw how Jesus gave them the time it took to build this kind of loving relationship, but also how he did *not* do this with everyone. They remembered that, at times, he left crying multitudes on the beach and struck off across the lake on a boat. Over the three years with him, the disciples witnessed Jesus' love in all phases of his life, yet he reserved a special kind of love for them.

Pastor and author Louis Evans Jr. put it this way: "Try to respond to every call and be all things to all people and there will be one result — worn out!"[6] This applied even to Jesus. We often forget this in stressing his divinity over his humanity. Yet, being fully human as well as fully divine, he was completely realistic about his earthly limitations. He knew there was no way he could love everyone in the same way. Knowing his limitations, he chose twelve individuals into whom he poured his love.

Stop to think what good news this is. What a much needed antidote for all of us who suffer from the guilties because we are not able to love everyone as we would like. The fact that Jesus loved realistically is a message to us saying, "Your time is finite. You do not have countless hours and energy to give to everyone. It is humanly impossible to give extravagantly of yourself to every person in your church, every person in your neighborhood, at your school, or at your office. Be realistic about how much you can give of yourself before becoming worn-out and ineffective."

Secondly, Jesus loved *intimately.* For three years, he and the disciples did everything together. They ate and slept together, cried and laughed together. They saw one another on their good days and bad days, and even before their morning cup of coffee!

Jesus lived and loved in this way, sharing himself totally with the twelve. Having him as our model, it is rather amazing that for the most part we have lost this sense of intimate loving in the church. Oh yes, there are a few congregations across the land that have followed Jesus' example, but for the most part, church members keep a safe distance from one another. I think of Bruce Larson's assessment of the church:

> I was a student minister at a little church up on the Hudson River — I'd go up every weekend from Princeton, where I was in seminary. I met my wife in that church, in fact. "Fellowship" consisted of a monthly meeting of the women's association and an occasional men's breakfast, where you had a baseball or football player come in and give his testimony.
>
> Then one weekend, I found out some shocking news: a teenage girl in the congregation had left town to go to her older brother's. She was pregnant. I said to the dear woman who told me, "Could I go and see her?"
>
> "Oh, no," she replied. "you're the last person she wants to know what's happened."
>
> Suddenly it hit me: That's what's wrong with the church in our time. It's the place you go when you put on your best clothes; you sit in Sunday school, you worship, you have a potluck dinner together — but you don't bring your life! You leave behind all your pain, your brokenness, your hopes, even your joys."[7]

We have allowed a counterfeit gospel to penetrate our lives — the Gospel of Rugged Individualism — rather than the Gospel of Jesus. The Gospel of Rugged Individualism tells us, "Don't let anyone get too close. Make it on your own. Sharing your hurts, doubts, and weaknesses is reserved for your family only."

How contrary to the Gospel of Christ. Even Jesus needed twelve people around him with whom he could be intimate. He fostered a ministry of closeness rather than of distance. Tragically, too many of us are like the man who had just repaired the sidewalk in front of his house. After making the repairs, the man stepped back to admire his work. A neighbor came by to admire it as well and, as they were talking, a man and his wife came walking down the street. The two passers-by were deeply engrossed in conversation and did not notice the wet cement. You guessed it. They stepped into it. As they did, the homeowner turned to his neighbor and said, "You know, I love people in general, but not in the concrete." Jesus calls us to an intimate, concrete love of one another.

Thirdly, Jesus loved *intentionally*. In Mark's gospel we read:

> Jesus went up on a mountainside and called to him those he wanted, and they came to him. He appointed twelve — designating them apostles — that they might be with him and that he might send them out to preach and to drive out demons (Mark 3:13–15, RSV).

Note two things here about Jesus. First, he chose to live in intimate fellowship with the disciples. In effect, Jesus was saying, "I have chosen you to be with me." He was very intentional about being in fellowship with the disciples. It did not happen coincidentally. He planned it and chose to make time for it.

Second, note the vehicle Jesus chose for living in intimate fellowship with the disciples. You are correct — a small group.

Now what does all this have to do with your small group? Just this — a healthy small group will be composed of those who, like Jesus, make their small group a high priority in their lives. Listen to the words of Roberta Hestenes:

> Although some groups choose to be casually structured and open to whoever shows up at a particular meeting, most groups discover a commitment to regular attendance is absolutely essential.

Sometimes people will say that they want to be in a small group but they have conflicting obligations which will require them to miss some of the meetings. This may be acceptable in some circumstances. Yet if the purpose of the group includes building relationships of love and care among the members, a floating population will make it difficult, if not impossible, to accomplish the group's purpose. Hard as it may be, those choosing to be in a group may have to alter or postpone, for the time being, some of their other commitments. When people share together in discussion and prayer, a level of trust is built up week by week. When some are absent or casual about their attendance, that building of trust is delayed or denied. Those for whom the group is a high priority may come to resent or shut out the less frequent attenders. Relationships need time and trust to develop. Those invited to join a group should be asked to commit themselves to attend each meeting until the end of the contract period.[8]

Jesus carved out time, gave up other things, to be with the disciples on a regular basis. He made himself available to them in a way he was not available to others. Was he being insensitive to the rest of the world or showing favoritism? No! He was just being realistic, intimate, and intentional with his love.

Did you ever throw a stone into a still lake? Between college and seminary, I spent my summers working at the YMCA camp in McCall, Idaho. It was situated on a gorgeous mountain lake. In early morning, before the campers awakened, I liked to sit on the lake shore and toss pebbles into the still, glassy water. The result was always the same — a series of ripples would spread where the pebble hit the water.

Think of the ripple effect Jesus' small group had on the world. As a result of his loving them *intentionally, realistically,* and *intimately,* the world was changed. Would Jesus' ministry have had as big an impact if he had not participated in a small group? We will never know, but apparently he did not think so. That is why he carved out time for the twelve.

Charles Schulz has illustrated this so very well. I chuckled when I read his cartoon, because Lucy accurately describes my erroneous approach to life:

Most of us are terrifically busy. Yet, do we give our energy to the things that matter? We move through life at the pace of a hydroplane cutting across the water, but what kind of ripples are we leaving? When Jesus had before him the task of bringing renewal to Israel, he formed a small group. He made it a high priority, knowing that love shared in the context of that small group would greatly impact the world. He had to give them extra time, turn away from other needs, but he determined it was worth it. So when we hear Jesus' command, "love one another," we must not forget the rest of the command, "... as I have loved you." How he loved the disciples is the way we are to love one another in the church — to invest ourselves intimately in the lives of a handful — not to run from the world's needs, but to better meet them.

When we participate in a small group, we are loving one another as Jesus expected us to love. When we make the group a high priority, only missing for illness or being out of town, we intentionally create the intimate sort of community Jesus had in mind for his people. When we say "yes" to small group life and "no" to other things, we are being realistic about our time and using it wisely, knowing that our small group can have a powerful ripple effect upon the world.

Are you willing to make that kind of commitment over the next ten weeks, be a regular attendee, and do the necessary reading and praying in preparation for each group meeting? Are you willing to make yourself available to your group in ways you are not to others? Even to take time to be with them in addition to your regular meetings?

If so, listen to Presbyterian pastor David Redding, who spoke of a retreat called Laity Lodge in his book *Jesus Makes Me Laugh*. Redding said, "People go there for the food and to get away to something churches used to be known for, but now rarely provide — a love that means giving yourself away to others until it hurts a little and makes you feel light-hearted."[9]

May we follow Jesus' example and love one another this way again.

STUDY TWO
Loving One Another

1. Check-In *(20–30 minutes)*

"Checking-in" provides an opportunity for group members to see how each is doing before moving to the study. It is a way to help members "get aboard," as well as demonstrate love for one another.

When we come to a meeting, we come with our joys and hurts. If we sit on these feelings, we can inadvertently short-circuit the meeting for ourselves and others. It takes an enormous amount of energy to sit on feelings. Some have likened it to holding a beach ball under water! "Checking-in" with one another at the beginning allows our beach ball to float to the surface and gives us the energy to be present to others in the group, rather than hold down our beach ball.

Here are some samples of check-in questions:

- What was the high point of your week and what was your low?
- If you could relive a part of your week, either because you enjoyed it or would like another chance at doing it over, what would you like to relive?
- How did you experience God in your life this past week?
- If you had to liken your mood tonight to a ride at an amusement park, it would be to a . . .

The best kind of check-in question for a group combines two elements:

- It allows members to share how they are feeling.
- It relates to the study theme.

This second aspect is not always possible, given the fact that some themes are easier to relate to than others. In terms of building loving relationships, if you have to choose between the two elements, choose the check-in question that will allow members to share their current feelings.

For your gathering this meeting, begin with this two-part question:

- When did you feel loved this week?
- When did you experience a lack of love?

The facilitator begins the sharing.

2. **Exploration** *(20–30 minutes)*
   a. Read John 13:31–35.
   b. Discuss the chapter. What surprised you? Troubled you? Challenged you? Comforted you? Ticked you off?
   c. What will you do as a group to make the group a high priority? How do you see this being lived out in practical and specific ways in relation to attendance, preparing for the meeting, and availability to one another?

3. **Sharing** *(45–55 minutes)*
   Take turns answering these questions:
   a. In addition to those in the group, to whom outside the group do you feel called to give of your quality time?
   b. How can the group be with you in prayer this coming week?

4. **Prayer** *(5 minutes)*
   Close with a sentence prayer for the person on your left:

   "Lord, thank you for _____ and be with him or her this week at _____ ."

   More will be said about prayer in the group in the next chapter.

5. **Assignment**
   Assign Chapter 3 for next week's reading.

CHAPTER **3**

Pray for One Another

*Therefore confess your sins
to one another,
and pray for one another
that you may be healed . . .*

James 5:16 (RSV)

I love the Los Angeles Dodgers. In fact, one of my fantasies is that someday the phone will ring and the manager of the Dodgers will ask me to serve as chaplain of the team. Such an experience would be a slice of heaven.

I did not always love the Dodgers, however. When I was a young boy, my favorite team was the New York Yankees. My favorite player was their center-fielder, Mickey Mantle, but close behind him was their catcher, Yogi Berra. Berra was one of the most colorful and popular players for the Yankees. He still remains one of the most quotable figures in sports, and a while ago Ben Patterson, a fellow Presbyterian pastor, reminded me of this in a magazine article about prayer.

One afternoon Yogi was involved in a tie ballgame, with two outs in the bottom of the ninth. An opposing batter stepped into the batter's box and proceeded to make the sign of the cross on home plate. Yogi, being a Catholic himself, noticed the act, wiped off the plate with his catcher's mitt, and said, "Why don't we let God just watch this game?"

In response to this classic Yogi comment, Patterson observed:

> That is good theology when applied to the outcome of a baseball game. It is terrible theology when applied to the way we live our lives and carry out the work of the church. Worse than that, it is fatal.
>
> But too often that is precisely the outlook we bring to our vocation.... God is in attendance at the game, but only as our honored spectator. Our prayers are merely ceremonial functions: tips of the hat, verbal recognition over the loudspeaker between innings, or requests to throw out the game ball. He even may have the best seat in the stadium, but he rarely, if ever, gets on the playing field."[1]

Is Patterson overstating things a bit? Not if we are to believe half of what we read in surveys concerning the weight and frequency given to prayer in the average Christian's life. A recent survey showed that an average layperson spends four minutes a day in prayer, while the usual pastor spends just seven minutes.

I shared those figures with an early morning small group I enable in which we study the Scripture passage from which I will be preaching the following week. Afterward, someone in the group commented, "No wonder there are so many dead churches!" I would add to that, "No wonder so many of us feel so out of touch with God."

Given the example of Christ's continual prayer life, why do *we* spend so little time in prayer? Jesus constantly went off by himself to pray, and at times spent the entire night in prayer. Why then do we pray so infrequently? Three possibilities come to mind.

1. We do not know how to pray.

We pray so little because, like the disciples, we wonder how to pray. Remember the request they made to Jesus?

> One day Jesus was praying in a certain place. When he finished, one of his disciples said to him, "Lord, teach us to pray, just as John taught his disciples."
> He said to them, "When you pray, say:
> 'Father, hallowed be your name,
> your kingdom come, may your will be done
> on earth as it is in heaven.
> Give us each day our daily bread.
> Forgive us our sins, for we also forgive those
> who sin against us.
> And lead us not into temptation.'
> (Luke 11:1–4, NIV)

Picture that scene. Jesus was at a slight distance from his disciples who were together, watching him pray. They realized how differently he prayed than they did. It was certainly a higher priority in his life. He often, as he was doing at that moment, went off alone to pray. And what results! Before long the disciples began making a connection between Jesus' public life and his prayer life. As they watched they talked about the spiritual bankruptcy in their own lives. Oh, if only they could pray like Jesus. If only they could sense God's power and presence in their lives as he did.

After a while one of them suggested, "Why don't we ask Jesus how to pray? After all, it's common for disciples to ask rabbis such questions. Let's ask him."

So they chose one of the group to speak for them, and when Jesus had finished praying, the selected disciple walked over to him and said, "Lord, teach us to pray."

Funny, but things have not changed much over the past centuries. We modern-day disciples of Christ have the same request. Many of us would love to pray like the Master. We do not want to live off the spiritual experience of another. We want first-hand conversation with our Creator and Sustainer. But, like the disciples, we do not know how to go about it.

Yet we can do something. We too can learn. In fact, learning how to pray for oneself and others is one of the more exciting aspects of small group life. In the weeks ahead the studies in this book will allow you to experiment with different kinds of prayer and ways of praying. If you are a novice at prayer, remember that God meets us where we are and moves us slowly into deeper waters.

2. We do not think prayer accomplishes much.

Another reason we pray so infrequently is that many of us do not believe prayer really accomplishes anything. I think of a seminar I lead on prayer at which I asked the participants why we do not pray more often. A very honest woman named Audrey responded, "Because, deep down, we don't think prayer really does much. We think it's a nice, religious thing to do, and it makes us feel better, but that's about all. If we really believed prayer got God's attention, our knees would have calluses. But they don't, because we don't believe prayer does all that much."

That is the problem, is it not? Many of us do not genuinely believe that prayer moves the hand of God. Our actions reveal our belief. Think for a moment. What usually happens in our lives when the pressures of family, friends, community activities, school, and work begin accumulating? Do we spend more — or less — time in prayer? How many of us would consider these words of Martin Luther, when swamped one day by demands on his time: "I have so much to do today, I need to spend two hours in prayer instead of one."

Was Luther crazy? No. He knew prayer moved the hand of God. He knew when he prayed he was doing something vitally important. So when pressure mounted, he knew the most important thing he could do was pray about it.

I usually do just the opposite. I am embarrassed to say, when faced with a demanding schedule, I cut my prayer time in half because I have so much to do. When that happens I need to remember another comment made by Presbyterian pastor Ben Patterson: "Many of us feel we have too much to do to have time to pray. That's the problem. At bottom we don't believe we are really doing anything when we pray."[2]

Ouch! The problem is that many of us see prayer as a luxury, icing on the cake, rather than a means of actually doing something. For example, it is fine to pray as a kind of warm-up exercise in intimacy with Christ and others, but pray to get things done? Not really. Ben Patterson rightly says that when we must get something done, prayer usually is cast aside so we can get to work talking, writing, telephoning, budgeting, or organizing. Prayer, for many of us, is a pleasant luxury. It would be nice to spend more time praying, but only if so many necessities did not press upon us. We think we are too busy to pray, when the truth is we are too busy because we have *not* prayed!

Jesus, though, saw prayer as his central task. Looking at his life, we are struck by the time he spent praying, especially given the demands he endured. Luke gives a classic example:

> Yet the news about him spread all the more, so that crowds of people came to hear him and to be healed of their sicknesses. But Jesus often withdrew to lonely places and prayed. (Luke 5:15–16, NIV)

Why did Jesus do something so crazy? Why not stay at work, preaching and healing? Why did he go off to pray instead?

Because, for him, prayer was his first obligation. It unleashed God's power in his life and the lives of others. Jesus knew if he did not fall on his knees, he would soon fall on his face.

3. We have a faulty concept of God.

A third reason we spend so little time in prayer lies with our concept of God. Note how Jesus addressed God in prayer as "Father." Understanding God as a loving, heavenly parent is so important in our attitude and approach, for how we picture God will influence what we expect of our Creator in prayer. For instance, a certain schoolboy was asked what he thought God was like. He replied that, as far as he could make out, God was "the sort of person who is always snooping round to see if people are enjoying themselves and then trying to stop it!"

If we, like this schoolboy, picture God as a cosmic kill-joy, then we will not go to God very often in prayer.

Then there are those who picture God at the other extreme, as a colossal vending machine, whose sole purpose is to give us what we want. Just pop in a prayer and out comes our heart's desire. A problem arises, however, when prayer does not work out quite so simply, when the expected results are not produced. Then, in disappointment and anger, we kick and scream at our cosmic vending machine for swallowing our prayer.

Jesus likens God to neither of these extremes. To him, God is like a good parent who will give us in prayer what is good for us, not always what we want.

I think back to a time when our family was vacationing on the Oregon coast. Our children were five and eight, and we spent the night in Florence, Oregon, located a few miles south of the Sea Lion Caves. The caves were great. The gift shops were a disaster. Have you ever noticed how low the shelves are in gift shops? They were the perfect height for our five-year-old, Jenny. And the shops were everywhere. There was one at our motel, another at the restaurant, and, of course, at the Sea Lion Caves. Needless to say, we battled our children at every one. "Mom, can I have this?" "Dad, what about this?"

We also found we were not alone in the battle. At the restaurant, in the midst of wrestling our children, my wife and I overheard a mother say to her young son as they were passing through the gift shop, "Keep your eyes straight ahead and keep moving!"

The point? As a father, at times I must say "no" to my children. If I always said "yes," they would become spoiled. Furthermore, they would be unprepared for life in the real world, where disappointment is a fact of life. Thankfully, our Heavenly Parent sometimes says "no" to us as well.

Can you imagine what it would be like if God gave us everything we asked for in prayer? Some of the best answers I have received have been "no." It has been suggested that if we thought all our requests were going to be granted simply because we asked — without the benefit of God's review or wisdom — there would probably be very few prayers we would dare to pray.

God oftentimes says "no," but also, many times, "yes." In the Sermon on the Mount Jesus instructed his listeners:

> Ask and it will be given to you; seek and you will find; knock and the door will be opened to you. For everyone who asks receives; he who seeks finds; and to him who knocks, the door will be opened.
>
> Which of you, if his son asks for bread, will give him a stone? Or if he asks for a fish, will give him a snake? If you, then, though you are evil, know how to give good gifts to your children, how much more will your Father in heaven give good gifts to those who ask him! So in everything, do to others what you would have them do to you, for this sums up the Law and the Prophets. (Matt. 7:7–12, NIV)

Our Heavenly Parent always has our best interests at heart.

A Call to Pray for One Another

Whatever our objections and hesitancies, they do not change the fact that we are called to pray, and specifically for one another. After the death and resurrection of Jesus, the Apostle

James became the leader of the church in Jerusalem. Listen to his call to prayer for one another:

> Therefore, confess your sins to each other and pray for each other so that you may be healed. The prayer of a righteous man is powerful and effective.
> Elijah was a man just like us. He prayed earnestly that it would not rain, and it did not rain on the land for three and a half years. Again he prayed, and the heavens gave rain, and the earth produced its crops. (James 5:16–18, NIV)

James makes two important statements about prayer in these verses. Number one, he says it is powerful and effective. As it has been said, "Be careful what you ask for when you pray because you are likely to get it!" Prayer indeed moves the hand of God. Number two, James stresses our interdependence as Christians: "Pray for each other so that you may be healed." Louis Evans Jr. has observed, "Certain things will not happen in another person's life unless we pray for him. We or a covenant partner may have a need which can be fulfilled only by God's power, and when we pray for someone we love, we make that power available to that person. This is our responsibility to one another."[3]

Why does God act in this way? Why are certain resources available to us only through the prayers of others? Think of the kind of people we would be if we did not need anyone else. We would be lonely, isolated, and perhaps proud. God wants us to be distinguished by sharing, caring, and compassion for one another. So, to combat our self-sufficient tendencies, God created us with a need for Deity and for each other. Prayer is the language that draws us closer to God and to one another.

Prayer in the Group

Knowing we should pray for one another is one thing. Actually making prayer a part of our group is another. Though it can be one of the most meaningful experiences we share, it also can be one of the scariest and most frustrating.

If we have never prayed out loud in public, the thought of praying for one another can be quite threatening, embarrassing us because we do not know what to say or how to say it. Furthermore, since we sometimes ascribe spiritual maturity to how well someone prays, we may fear others will think less of us because of the way we pray. All this makes us want to run and hide when group prayer is mentioned.

Prayer in a small group also can be incredibly frustrating. At one time it was my least favorite part of our small group meeting. I dreaded the thought of it each week. It was not because I did not believe in prayer. I did. And I do. Wholeheartedly. In fact, I was very good about praying daily for the people in my group during the week. It was just when we were together that I disliked praying. The problem for me was that the format for the prayer was the same every week. We devoted the last fifteen minutes of our gathering to prayer, so when the clock signaled, we would religiously (no pun intended) do five things: gather in a circle, join hands, assign someone to begin the prayer, proceed clockwise around the circle praying for the concerns mentioned during the sharing time, and end with an appropriate closing by the last person.

I had two problems with this. One, sometimes my nose itched, or my arm started hurting, embarrassing me if I had to seek relief by letting go of the person's hand next to me. Thus I became increasingly concerned about my physical comfort, rather than the prayer intention. All I wanted was for the prayer time to end so that I could get comfortable again.

My other problem or frustration with this prayer method involved my contribution. Here is what normally happened. As the group proceeded around the circle, I spent considerable time thinking and composing my prayer. I wanted to be ready when it was my turn. Unfortunately, I often experienced the person just before me "stealing" my prayer! Panic would set in as I wondered for what or whom I should then pray!

Praying in a group does not need to be embarrassing or frustrating, however. Varying the ways of group prayer and being sensitive to one another's comfort level can make prayer an enriching experience for you and your group. Following are ways you might pray together over the weeks ahead. You have already practiced the first two together.

Some Methods of Group Prayer

Silent Prayer: Set aside two to ten minutes. Invite group members to close their eyes, silently thank God for being present, and individually pray for each group member. The time-keeper closes with "Amen," or a brief, verbal prayer or song.

Circle Prayer: Sit or stand in a circle. (Holding hands is optional!) Instruct each person to pray for the person on the left. Choose someone to begin, and proceed around the circle. The advantage is no one will pray for the same concern and everyone will be certain for whom they are praying.

Conversational Prayer: Someone begins by praying for one specific request. Whoever goes next (this is not done in a circle) prays for the same thing, then adds another specific request. The next person picks up the *new* request, then adds another. For example, Judy starts by praying for Margaret's job interview tomorrow. John, who goes next, also prays for Margaret, and then prays for Linda's relationship with her teenage daughter. The next person who feels called to pray begins with the intention for Linda, then offers another prayer for a person or situation that has been mentioned in the group. This continues until the person chosen to close with a prayer does so.

Designated Prayer: If you are short on time, one, two, or three people are assigned to close the group in prayer.

Popcorn Prayer: The enabler begins by simply saying, "Lord, we bring before you these joys and concerns." Members suggest prayer intentions as they are moved to. One word, name, or short phrase is mentioned at a time. The group may take ten or fifteen seconds between each intention to pray silently for the joys or concerns brought to mind.

Praying Our Concerns: If a group has separate times for prayer and for sharing prayer *requests*, members occasionally may want to eliminate the requests time, and simply make their needs known during the process of prayer itself. Thus, instead of Mike at sharing time mentioning his need for prayer while he travels, he would pray for that during the prayer time. In this way members would discover how to pray for each other during the week.

STUDY THREE
Praying for One Another

1. **Check-in** *(20–30 minutes)*
   With the enabler or leader going first, take turns responding to this two-part question:

   - What was the place of prayer in your home as a child?
   - Where were you in the need of prayer this past week?

2. **Exploration** *(20–30 minutes)*
   Discuss the reading. What grabbed you? What confused you? What comforted you? What bothered you?

3. A Prayer Experiment *(15 minutes)*

The leader brings out a box or ʾat containing the names of group members on separate and folded pieces of paper. Members are invited to draw a name (other than their own) and put the paper on their bathroom mirror, car dashboard, or refrigerator door as a reminder to pray for that person during the next five weeks, thanking God for him or her, asking for protection and guidance, and supporting in prayer the specific concerns voiced in the group by that person. After five weeks, you will share the experience of what it meant to pray for the person and be prayed for by another. (Time will be set aside for this in Chapter Eight. If your group is not meeting weekly, you may need to plan for this before or after the eighth session.)

4. Prayer Concerns *(30–40 minutes)*

Share one or two ways you would like to be supported in prayer this week.

5. Prayer *(5 minutes)*

Try using the "popcorn prayer" method mentioned in this chapter.

6. Assignment

Assign Chapter 4 for next week's reading.

CHAPTER

Care for One Another

But God has so composed the body,
giving the greater honor
to the inferior part,
that there may be no discord
in the body,
but that the members may have
the same care for one another.

I Corinthians 12:24b–25 (RSV)

"Caring and Sharing Together." That is how our congregation has chosen to describe itself. We painted those words on the sign in front of our church, and we also include them in our church advertising. Every Saturday morning they appear on the church page of the newspaper, and if someone is looking for a church home, that is what we hope they will find and do here: Care and share.

I wonder how First Church Corinth would have advertised itself in the Saturday morning edition of The Corinthian Daily News? Somehow I do not think they would have chosen "Caring and Sharing Together," since that hardly would have captured the essence of who they were.

One thing for which I am eternally grateful is that the Lord did not call me to pastor First Church Corinth. Talk about a wild and woolly bunch! What a church. I like the way Russell Spittler describes it in his brief commentary on Paul's Letter to the Corinthians:

> Imagine a church like this one:
> Members sue each other before civil courts. Others habitually attend social banquets honoring strange gods, mere idols. One brother lives in open immorality — and the church tolerates it. Others think it would be better for Christian couples to separate so they could be more "holy."
> Their worship services are shocking, anything but edifying. Speakers in tongues show no restraints. People come drunk to the Lord's Supper, where they shy off into exclusive groups — each bragging about its favorite preacher. Visitors get the impression they are mad.
> Some doubt the Resurrection. And many have reneged on their financial pledges.
> Was there ever such a church? Yes. What's more, its founder and pastor for a year and a half was the Apostle Paul!"[1]

I guess that is why Paul penned the words "care for one another" in his first letter to the church at Corinth:

> But God has so composed the body, giving the greater honor to the inferior part, that there be no discord in the body, but that the members may have the same care for one another. If one member suffers, all suffer together; if one member is honored, all rejoice together. (I Cor. 12: 24b-25, RSV)

The Corinthians were far from caring. In fact, Paul's entire chapter was written to comfort those made to feel unwanted in the church. Members were saying things like, "If you do not have certain gifts then you are really not vital to the church"; "Our gifts are better than your gifts"; and, "If you do not have the gifts we have then you have not arrived yet in Jesus Christ." Instead of "Caring and Sharing Together," the church at Corinth would better be known as "Screaming and Demeaning Together." I do not know how Paul persisted with them. I guess that is why he is called *Saint* Paul.

Webster's New World Dictionary defines "care for" as: "1) to love or to like. 2) to wish for; want. 3) to take charge of; look after; provide for."[2] How would we apply these definitions and go about caring for one another in a small group?

Let me suggest four ways. Two take place during the meeting, and two between meetings.

Caring During the Meeting

One way we care for one another is through attentive listening. One cannot underestimate the symbiotic relationship between feeling cared for and being listened to. For example, listen to the words of M. Scott Peck, Morton Kelsey, Paul Tournier . . . and Charles Schulz:

> *M. Scott Peck*: "The principle form that the word of love takes is attention. When we love another we give him or her our attention; we attend to that person's growth. . . . By far the most common and important way in which we can exercise our attention is by listening."[3]

Morton Kelsey: "It is impossible for us to love other people unless we listen. We simply cannot love without learning to listen."[4]

Paul Tournier: "It is impossible to overemphasize the immense need humans have to be really listened to, to be taken seriously, to be understood. No one can develop freely in the world and find life without feeling understood by at least one person."[5]

Charles Schulz:

Unfortunately there are a lot of Lucys out there. Can you identify with Charlie Brown? It is amazing how regularly we fail to listen. Take the woman who said to her friend, "Talk, talk, talk. That's all my husband ever does is talk, talk, talk."

The friend asked, "Well, what does he talk about?"

"I don't know, he doesn't ever say."

The trouble is we have been *saying*, but few have been *listening*. I am reminded of the Zen teacher who was visited by a student. The teacher invited the student to stay for a while and have tea. After they were seated the Zen master poured the cup full, then allowed it to overflow onto the table and to the floor. The student finally yelled, "Stop! Why do you do this?"

The teacher said, "So it is with you. You are so full of your own preoccupations there is no room for anything new to enter."

In this regard, George Parsons of the Alban Institute tells of a meeting he and others from the Institute had with John McDonald, an ambassador to three countries during his career and the head of the State Department's Foreign Affairs Institute. (This is a "mini-university" attended by diplomats as part of their training.) At the end of the meeting, McDonald said something very interesting about Americans. If he could gather together in one room the representatives of the world's forty largest nations (by gross national product), and give them a test to see what kind of listeners they were, McDonald was convinced the American representatives would rate fortieth. He said, "Americans are known around the world by their inability to listen."[6]

Listening

As the weeks go by for this group, we can learn to do a better job of listening to one another. Here are some ways to improve listening skills:

1. Give the appearance of listening.
Look interested. Tapping a pencil, humming a tune, gazing out the window, doing needlepoint, or thumbing through a book hardly appears attentive.

2. Use your eyes.
Sixty percent of communication is nonverbal (gestures, body posture, facial expressions). The tone of voice conveys an additional 33%. Actual words make up only 7% of what we are trying to communicate. In the immortal words of Flip Wilson's Geraldine, "What you see is what you get!" Pick up on nonverbal signs.

3. Learn to concentrate.
We think faster than people speak, on the average four or five times faster. It is natural, then, that our

minds wander as we listen. When you find yourself mentally "leaving the room," gently call yourself back to the person speaking.

4. Avoid interrupting.
Sometimes it is necessary to intervene, especially when someone is speaking ad nauseam, oblivious to others. For the most part, though, interrupt only to clarify, not to change the focus. Comments like, "I know what you mean," or "My Uncle Harry had that happen to him too," shifts the focus to someone else.

5. Clarify messages.
What you hear is not necessarily what the other person said or meant to say. You can break up potential log jams and clarify meanings by repeating what you think you heard, "I heard you say..." or by asking, "Is this what you are saying?" Make sure you understand the message before sharing your own perceptions and feelings in response.

6. Develop the gift of brevity in speech.
Avoid talking non-stop for long periods of time. Choose words that are few and full. Give others time to talk.

Caring, Not Curing
A second way to care for one another during group meetings is to care, *not cure*.

A few years ago I attended a Faith at Work Leadership Training Institute. Our welcome packet included a green sheet of paper, headed "MAY WE SUGGEST." Under the heading were guidelines offered to help the Institute benefit all the participants in the small group. I do not know who authored the suggestions, but I sensed they were born out of years of painful small group experiences.

At the top of the list, guideline number one was: "It is more blessed to CARE than to CURE." I had heard that for years, but it registered then for the first time. Why did it finally make sense to me as I prepared for the Institute? Because I had shortly before witnessed two incidents leading to the carnage of ignoring that guideline.

One incident involved a woman in her mid-thirties. We had been together in a group two days before. As we shared our responses to a relational Bible study question, she began to cry. Fighting back tears, she went on to say that she was tired of taking care of people and having no one to care for her. "I have gobs of friends," she said, "but none of them really listen to me. Whenever I share the pain in my life, I immediately receive advice like, 'Have you done this?' or 'Have you tried that?' or 'If I were you, here's what I would do.' For once, for once, would someone just listen, without trying to fix me?"

Our group sat in silence as she gave way to her tears.

The other incident involved a women about fifty years old. We were engaged in a one-on-one conversation. She was insightful, beautiful, vivacious, and concerned about her age. She shared her opinion that aging is kinder to men than to women, at least according to our society. Married to a physically attractive, successful, powerful attorney, she wondered if she would be able to keep him interested in her. "After all," she said, "power is an aphrodisiac, and does my husband ever exude power!"

She then stopped talking and her eyes began to redden. I could see the fear and pain in her eyes.

I almost said, "Oh, Jane [a pseudonym], don't worry about it. It's what is inside that counts. Your husband would be crazy to ever walk away from you."

Instead, by the grace of God, before the words left my mouth, I began to cry. As the tears filled my eyes and ran down my cheeks, she hugged me and said, "Thank you for understanding. People usually tell me, 'Don't worry. You have nothing to fear.'"

Thank goodness those words never left my mouth.

When I share the pain in my life, I want people to love me, to hold me, to understand me. If I want advice, I will ask for it. I will long remember how bothered I became a couple of years ago after sharing with a group my concerns about letting my schedule get away from me. My day off was being interrupted. I was spending way too many hours on the job, and the people who helped me least were those who said, "Why don't you take off Monday instead?" or "Go away on your day off so you won't be bothered" or "Don't go to so many committee meetings."

I knew they were trying to help lessen my pain by giving me some options. The only problem was, I had explored those options and what I did not want was more advice. What I wanted was to let people know where I was struggling so that they could specifically pray for me. That was all.

The following poem says it well. I do not know who wrote it. It is entitled, "Listen to Me."

> When I ask you to listen to me
>   and you start giving advice,
>   you have not done what I asked.
>
> When I ask you to listen to me
>   and you begin to tell me why
>   I shouldn't feel that way
> you are tramping on my feelings.
>
> When I ask you to listen to me
>   and you feel you have to do something
>   to solve my problem,
> you have failed me, strange as that may seem....
>
> When you do something for me
>   that I can and need to do for myself,
> you contribute to my fear and weakness.
>
> But when you accept as a simple fact
>   that I do feel what I feel,
>   no matter how irrational,
>   then I can quit trying to convince you

and get about the business of understanding
what's behind this irrational feeling.
And when that's clear,
   the answers can become obvious
   and I won't need advice....

"It is more blessed to care than to cure." I do not think it appeared on top of the green sheet by accident. For attempting to cure, rather than care, is probably the most common mistake made by group members in their attempt to hear and respond to people they love.

Over the years I have collected some "cure" statements and some "care" statements. Some typical ones are:

CURE STATEMENTS

"Don't worry. It will work out."
"Have you tried . . ."
"I struggled with that once too. It will pass."
"Why don't you . . ."
"My Aunt Paula faced a similar situation, and here is
   what she did."

CARE STATEMENTS

"How can I support you in this?"
"That sounds painful." (or hard or frustrating)
"Thank you for sharing that part of you with me."
"I wish I could do something. I feel so helpless."
"Is it OK to call you in a couple of days and see how
   you are doing with this?"

Get the picture? It may be hard to believe, but caring facilitates curing.

Caring Between Meetings

A small group becomes a caring group when the caregiving extends beyond the designated meeting times. This shows itself in two ways.

Number one: Group members do practical, helpful things for one another during the week. By that I mean they help each other with house-sitting, child-care, car repairs, and the like. In this regard I think of Gwen, a single woman in our group who helps my wife and me with house-sitting and cares for our dog when we travel. I think also of the time our group helped Bill and Becky move into their new home. Then there is all the traveling we do, going to weddings of children of group members. We have traveled hundreds of miles to be with one another during these poignant times of life. Moreover, everyone of us at one time has called another member at mid-week, sometimes in the middle of the night, to talk during a crisis in our lives.

Number two: Group members care for one another between meetings by committing themselves to pray daily for one another. During the group sharing time, they jot down the prayer requests on a sheet of paper, then post them in a prominent place to help remember group members in prayer.

Mother Theresa was asked, "What are the sources of your strength?"

She replied, "A 98-year-old woman in Philadelphia who prays for me."[7]

When we pray for one another between meetings, Christ's love flows through us to the other person. Daily, intercessory prayer is one of the greatest acts of caring we can express to those whom God has given us to love. Thank God for little old women in Philadelphia, and little old men in Omaha, and young women and young men everywhere, who are praying for us daily. That includes the members of our small group.

STUDY FOUR
Caring for One Another

1.   **Check-In** (20–30 minutes)
     Share your answers to the following questions with the group:

     • Outside of your immediate family, who is one of the best listeners you know?

• Who really listened to you this past week?

2. **Exploration** *(30 minutes)*
   a. Discuss the chapter. What struck you? Challenged you? Offended you? Confused you? Excited you?
   b. Discuss the four suggested ways you can care for one another in your small group. Which do you want to work on in the weeks ahead?
   (Enabler: Encourage each person to share one of the four, why they chose it, and how they hope to apply it to their life.)

3. **Prayer Concerns** *(30–45 minutes)*
   As members share their concerns, work on active listening and caring (not curing).

4. **Prayer** *(10–15 minutes)*
   Try using the conversational prayer method mentioned in the previous chapter.

5. **Assignment**
   Assign Chapter 5 for next week's reading.

CHAPTER

Bear

Bear
One
Another's
Burdens

(Self-Disclosure)

Bear one another's burdens,
and so fulfil the law of Christ.

Galatians 6:2 (RSV)

In the *Communicator's Commentary* Maxie Dunham reminds us of an event from Truman Capote's *Other Voices, Other Rooms.* The hero is about to walk along a heavy but rotting beam over a brooding, murky creek. Capote wrote, "...stepping gingerly...he felt he would be balanced here, suspended between land and in the dark and alone. Then feeling the board shake as Idabel started across, he remembered that he had someone to be together with. And he could go on."

Dunham, reflecting upon that event said, "Isn't this our experience? It certainly has been mine. I shiver at the thought of having to go it alone. I get chills when I consider where I might be if at the right time I had not felt the board shake because someone was walking with me!"[1]

We can be thankful that the Christian journey is a shared experience. We are not to go it alone. The Apostle Paul tells us to "bear one another's burdens" (Gal. 6:2, RSV). In other words, help or aid one another along the way. The word Paul uses for "bear" is very descriptive. It literally refers to the act of carrying a soldier's pack. It is a graphic picture! We are to help each other carry the things that weigh us down. In fact, some translations of the Bible have changed the more familiar and traditional word "bear" to "carry," in an attempt to more faithfully approximate the original Greek text.

In this and the next chapter, we will investigate the implications of this "one another" directive for small group life. In this chapter we will look at the importance of self-disclosure as it relates to bearing one another's burdens. Simply put, we cannot bear one another's burdens if we do not know what they are. If I do not tell you what I need help carrying, how can you help me carry it? In the next chapter we will discuss the importance of confidentiality as it relates to bearing one another's burdens. After all, I am not about to tell you how you can help me unless I feel I can trust you with that privileged information from my life.

Jesus and Self-Disclosure

Back in 1985 I clipped a short article out of the *Omaha World-Herald*. It contained some advice which the then mayor of Omaha, Mike Boyle, had received from some third graders. As a class project, the children at Sandoz Elementary School were to write the mayor suggesting ways he might spend tax dollars more efficiently.

One pupil wrote, "I would like more food invented because I almost have the same thing every day."

Another third grader proposed that the city do more for "old people that don't have any money." She wrote, "Just a little more money pretty please. But don't add anything else to the schools because we're tortchered [that's how she spelled it!] enough."

My favorite, though, came from one junior citizen to His Honor the Mayor: "Do you have probmals? [Yes, that's how he spelled it.] Are there probmals you can't solve? There are some for me that I can't solve around where I live. I'm glad you are the mayor. Probmals that people can't solve you solve them."

Probmals (or problems) — we all have them. As someone said, "Whenever you sit next to someone you sit next to a problem." We may cover them up pretty well, we might put on a good act, but they are there. Even Jesus had them. In fact, one problem had him sweating blood.

> They went to a place called Gethsemane, and Jesus said to his disciples, "Sit here while I pray." He took Peter, James, and John along with him, and he began to be deeply distressed and troubled. "My soul is overwhelmed with sorrow to the point of death," he said to them. "Stay here and keep watch."
>
> Going a little farther, he fell to the ground and prayed that if possible the hour might pass from him. "Abba, Father," he said, "everything is possible for you. Take this cup from me. Yet not what I will, but what you will."
>
> Then he returned to his disciples and found them sleeping. "Simon," he said to Peter, "are you

asleep? Could you not keep watch for one hour? Watch and pray so that you will not fall into temptation. The spirit is willing, but the body is weak."

Once more he went away and prayed the same thing. When he came back, he again found them sleeping, because their eyes were heavy. They did not know what to say to him.

Returning the third time, he said to them, "Are you still sleeping and resting? Enough! The hour has come. Look, the Son of Man is betrayed into the hands of sinners. Rise! Let us go! Here comes the betrayer!" (Mark 14:32–42, NIV)

"Thug Thursday" I call it. It was the night of Jesus' arrest. He was soon taken to prison and beaten, and he waited in a place called Gethsemane. The name is a forewarning in itself. Gethsemane literally means "press," denoting the stomping of a grape to squeeze the juice from a vine. It would not be long before Jesus had the life squeezed out of him.

Gethsemane was a private garden. In Jerusalem at the time there were no city parks like those in our communities today. A strange law in Jerusalem stated that the city's sacred soil must not be polluted with manure.

Somehow, however, the rich got around the law with private gardens for rest and relaxation. Apparently Jesus had a wealthy friend who allowed him the use of one. Luke tells us in his gospel that Jesus came there often to pray and be refreshed and renewed. Judas knew this and led Roman soldiers straight to him.

A particularly interesting aspect to this story was Jesus' emotional state while waiting in the garden. Note how Mark describes Jesus' condition shortly after coming to the garden. He says Jesus "began to be deeply distressed and troubled" (Mark 14:33, NIV). Actually this is an antiseptic translation of the Greek. A more exact account would be, "He began to be terrified and disoriented."

Moreover, note Christ's own description of his emotional state: "My soul is overwhelmed with sorrow to the point of death" (Mark 14:34, NIV). Such a Jesus may disappoint some of us. We intrude into Jesus' private agony as if peeping through a keyhole, observing him at his most vulnerable moment. Even though we affirm in our confessions of faith that Jesus was *fully human* and *fully divine*, we most often have greater difficulty with his humanity than his divinity.

Not only that, we do not like to see our super-heroes seemingly falter. Of course, some skeptics have criticized Jesus here, claiming other martyrs faced death more courageously. Yet remember that Jesus was not dying for a momentary cause or another person, but for the sins of the world. In a short time he would have the sins of murder, stealing, pride, gossip, and rape heaped upon him. For a crucial moment in history he, who did none of those things, would be guilty of them all in order to reconcile us with God.

What came next describes Jesus' emotional state even more vividly: "Going a little farther, he fell to the ground and prayed that if possible the hour might pass from him" (Mark 14:35, NIV).

The Greek that Mark uses here to describe Christ's actions is in the imperfect verb tense, indicating that Jesus' falling and praying were continual and constant. He did not fall to the ground and pray just once, but fell to the ground and prayed, stood up, walked a few yards, fell again and prayed, stood up once more, walked around, fell to the ground again and prayed. That is the scene. Under the moonlight the soon-to-be crucified Christ was moving about, driven by the anguish of his soul.

And the prayer that he repeated again and again and again, under great travail, was "Abba ["Daddy" in the Aramaic], Father, everything is possible for you. Take this cup from me. Yet not what I will, but what you will" (Mark 14:36, NIV).

The picture Mark paints is Jesus fighting to surrender. Jesus prayed the prayer of surrender. He thought he had surrendered, then boom, the terror struck again and he fell to the ground and prayed the prayer once more. Again and again this scene repeated itself. The fear of suffering and of the unknown, the thought of being separated from his Heavenly Parent robbed Jesus of the peace and confidence that normally characterized him.

Fear. Chuck Swindoll says of it in *Growing Strong in the Seasons of Life*:

> Fear. Ever met this beast? Sure you have. It creeps into your cockpit by a dozen different doors. Fear of failure. Fear of heights. Fear of crowds. Fear of disease. Fear of rejection. Fear of unemployment. Fear of what others are saying about you. Fear of moving away. Fear of height or depth or distance or death. Fear of being yourself. Fear of buying. Fear of selling. Fear of financial reversal. Fear of war. Fear of the dark. Fear of being alone.
>
> Lurking in the shadows around every imaginable corner, it threatens to poison your inner peace and outward poise. Bully that it is, the creature relies on scare tactics and surprise attacks. It watches for your vulnerable moment, then picks the lock that safeguards your security. Once inside, it strikes quickly to transform spiritual muscle into mental mush.[2]

But look how the story ends. After all the up and down praying, Jesus returned to the disciples and said, "Are you still sleeping and resting? Enough! The hour has come! Look, the Son of Man is betrayed into the hands of sinners. Rise! Let us go! Here comes my betrayer!" (Mark 14:41–42, NIV).

The fog and fear that had crept into his life was gone. Why? Three reasons come to mind. One, he faced his fear. He did not hide his fear, deny it, or run from it. He named it, fighting it face to face.

Two, he prayed about it. Remember the lines of the old hymn?

> Oh what peace we often forfeit
> Oh what needless pain we bear
> All because we do not carry
> Everything to God in prayer.[3]

Thirdly, Jesus shared his fear with the disciples. He was open with them about his struggle and asked for their help. "My soul is overwhelmed with sorrow to the point of death. Stay here and keep watch" (Mark 14:34, NIV). Of course, they could have done a better job of bearing his burden. Jesus even told them so. When he found them asleep, he cried out, "Simon, are you asleep? Could you not keep watch for one hour?" (Mark 14:37, NIV).

I am reminded of an episode of the television sit-com "Taxi." Alex had been mugged and shot by one of his passengers and when he returned to work he was afraid to get back in the cab. Afraid he might get shot again, he shared his fear with his cabby buddies. They listened, attempted to dispel his fear, encouraged him, and finally persuaded him to get back in the cab and pick up his first passenger. They told him, "Do it and you'll feel better. It will be okay."

Reluctantly, he took to the street, but drove around looking for someone safe to pick up. He finally spotted a priest who got into the cab and told Alex where he wanted to be taken. Alex became nervous. It was a poor, tough section of town, and he began wondering if his passenger was really a priest. So he asked the man, "Are you sure you are a priest? You look too young to be a priest."

"Yes," the passenger answered, "I am a priest."

Still not convinced, Alex asked, "Say, the other day some of us were talking about the twelve disciples and we couldn't remember all their names. Can you fill in the blanks for us?"

The priest said, "Sure," and began naming them. "Let's see. There was Peter, James, Andrew, John, Matthew...ah, Judas..." With that, there was a pause while the priest tried to remember all the names. But with the silence Alex slammed on the brakes and made the priest get out. He was convinced the man was only masquerading as a priest, trying to lull Alex into a false sense of security in order to rob him.

The point? Friends may fall asleep on us, as did the disciples with Jesus, and our friends might not totally dispel our irrational fears, as was the case with Alex's friends (he was still scared to death of potential muggers), but overall, sharing our fears and problems with others helps us deal with struggles and overcome them.

Self-Disclosure and Small Group Life

It is tough to say, "I need you." It is difficult to admit our needs for a variety of reasons. One is our upbringing. Do any of these ring a bell for you?

"Only the strong survive."
"Keep a stiff upper lip."
"Tough it out."
"When the going gets tough, the tough get going."
"Nobody wants to hear your problems. People have
   enough problems of their own."
"Big boys don't cry."

Unless we were raised by wolves in the wilderness, hardly a day went by when we did not get one of those messages at home or school, on the radio or television. Our society has taught us (especially men) to be self-sufficient and rugged.

In a 1982 *Newsweek* column about male friendships, Eliot Engle tells about getting ready to move cross country to a new teaching position. Just before he and his wife left town, her best friend came for a final good-bye. Eliot watched the women and described the scene like this: "Their last hugs were so painful to witness that I finally had to turn away and leave the room. I've always been amazed at the nurturing emotional support my wife can seek and return with her close female friends. Her three-hour talks with friends refresh her and renew her far more than my three-mile jogs restore me. In our society it seems as if you've got to have a bosom to be a buddy."[4]

Most men find friendship hard. When the leading psychologists and therapists in the country were asked, "How many men have real friends," they answered, "Ten percent," The conversations most males have with one another are a travesty. Men have safe "doing-things-together" friends, like golfing, fishing or jogging buddies, but generally no friends with whom they share their thoughts and feelings. Men have been told through the years not to do it, and they got the message.

It also is difficult to admit our needs and ask for help, because we fear ridicule. I ache for Charlie Brown.

Father John Powell asks, *Why Am I Afraid to Tell You Who I Am?*[5] We are afraid for a number of reasons: People might think less of us; people might make fun of us and our concerns; or people might use what they know about us against us.

There are risks, however, in not allowing others to know us. One is loneliness. Another is bewilderment. Nathaniel Hawthorne said it well: "No man can for any considerable time wear one face to himself and another to the multitude without finally getting bewildered as to which is the true one."

A turning point in my life took place the summer of 1986. We had just occupied our new sanctuary after a building project that had taken five long, hard years. During the last year we were short-handed, and I was the only pastor remaining on the staff, where we previously had had three. Furthermore, it was a controversial venture, as are most building projects. It had its highs and lows.

Toward the end, however, I began noticing something strange. I began to fear getting into the pulpit — nothing major at first, just low-level anxiety. Yet as the weeks passed it got worse. Then early on a Sunday morning, the day before we were to go on vacation, the fear seemed unbearable. I asked my wife if she would call in sick for me. I was afraid to preach. She told me I needed to make the call myself. She would not do it for me. So I forced myself to preach the sermon and then left for vacation, thinking all I needed was a little rest.

After three weeks' rest I returned, hoping my condition had improved. It had not. Not sure what to do, and thinking I might need to leave professional ministry, I called a meeting of the session (our church board) and asked them if I could take a month off without pay. I told them of my fear, that I needed counseling, and thought my ministry was over.

The session members were understanding and compassionate. They said "no" to my request for one month off without pay. Instead, I was encouraged to take three months off with pay. They told me I had been working way too hard. They had seen it coming and they asked for my forgiveness. Can you imagine!

I took the time, but not all of it. I took two months instead of three. I rested, read, and saw a terrific therapist. I came back renewed, invigorated, ready to preach, but wondering if anyone would want to listen to a preacher who had some chinks in his armor. I was sure worship attendance would drop. The opposite happened. Attendance increased and so did my counseling load! Individual after individual who came to see me for counseling said, "I decided to come because I knew you would understand. You know what it means to hurt and to fail."

I think this is something of what the Apostle Paul was struggling with when he referred to Christ's words, "My power is made perfect in weakness" (II Cor. 12:9, NIV).

Being open and honest about our struggles and pains is a gift. It is a gift to God for it gives God room to operate in our lives. As Vance Havner said,

> "God uses broken things.
> Broken soil to produce a crop,
> broken clouds to give rain,
> broken grain to give bread,
> broken bread to give strength.
> It is the broken alabaster box
> that gives forth perfume. It is Peter,

weeping bitterly, who returns to
greater power than ever."[6]

In other words, some of God's best work is with broken people. Not only that, it is usually our weakness that drives us to prayer in the first place. For this reason, weakness is a blessing, not a curse, for it brings us to our knees and gives God room to work in our lives.

Sharing our weakness also can be a gift to others. A case in point: A few weeks ago I was having lunch with a man in his forties. In the space of forty-five minutes, he told me (in capsulized form) the story of his life and his present hurts, fears, and questions. I felt like I was on holy ground. He allowed me to venture into the raw and real territory of his life. After lunch, on the way to our cars, he turned and said to me, "I'm sorry I burdened you with all this."

People say this to me all the time, but the opposite is always true. I answered him, "No, you did not burden me at all. You just gave me the greatest gift of all, the gift of yourself. Thank you for trusting me with who you really are."

Tragically, our fear of not being liked or accepted keeps us from giving the gift of ourselves to others. Are you willing to give that gift to the others in your group? And are you willing to accept that gift from others as well?

The blind songwriter Ken Medema wrote in one of his songs:

If this is not a place where tears are understood
    Then where shall I go to cry?
And if this is not a place
    where my spirit can take wings
    Then where shall I go to fly?
I don't need another place
    for tryin' to impress you
With just how good and virtuous I am,
    no, no, no.
I don't need another place
    for always bein' on top of things

Everybody knows that it's a sham,
    it's a sham.
I don't need another place
    for always wearin' smiles
Even when it's not the way I feel.
I don't need another place
    to mouth the same old platitudes
Everybody knows that it's not real.
So if this is not a place
    where my questions can be asked
      Then where shall I go to seek?
And if this is not a place
    where my heart cry can be heard
Where, tell me where, shall I go to speak?[7]

I hope that Ken and others like him could go to your small group. Creating an atmosphere where self-disclosure and openness are welcome is a prerequisite for being able to bear one another's burdens.

STUDY FIVE
Bearing One Another's Burdens (Self-Disclosure)

1.   **Check-In** *(20–30 minutes)*
    Disclose three things about yourself:
        • What game did you enjoy playing during your elementary years?
        • Who received your first romantic kiss?
        • What does the group need to know about your mood as the meeting begins?

2.   **Exploration** *(20 minutes)*
    Discuss the reading. What surprised you? Challenged you? Comforted you? Confused you? Bothered you?

3.   **Sharing** *(45–60 minutes)*
Enabler, have group members complete this sentence:

> "What keeps me from sharing myself
> with you or others is . . ."

The enabler's self-disclosure is very important in this and all small group exercises. Sometimes the process is called modeling. In modeling, the enabler goes first and "models" or gives an example of how the question is to be answered. If the enabler gives a surface type of answer, the group is likely to follow that lead. If the enabler gives a brief answer, the group is likely to do so. If the enabler answers in great detail, so will the group. The first person to share his or her answer to a question often provides the tone for the rest of the answers. As an enabler, make sure your answer is appropriate to the sharing level of the group. We can inhibit self-disclosure in one of two ways: by not revealing enough of ourselves, thus causing others to hold back; or by revealing too much, thus scaring people off who are not ready to share at that level.

After everyone has had a chance to complete the sentence, share prayer concerns.

4.   **Prayer** *(5–10 minutes)*
In this session and following sessions, pick a style of prayer that works for you and your group. You might want to vary the way you close in prayer, however, so as not to get into a rut.

5.   **Assignment**
Assign Chapter 6 for next week's reading.

6

Bear

One

Another's

Burdens

(Confidentiality)

Bear one another's burdens,
and so fulfil the law of Christ.

Galatians 6:2 (RSV)

"Pastor, your ten o'clock counseling session and last Sunday's sermon illustration are here!"

"Did you hear the latest about Mary?"

"Keep this to yourself. I don't mean to gossip, but . . ."

"I know I shouldn't be telling you this, but . . ."

"Fred, do you have a minute? I can't keep this to myself any longer."

"I heard through the grapevine that Janice was fired from her job. Is that true?"

CONFIDENTIALITY. It is the other prerequisite for bearing one another's burdens. We will not be comfortable disclosing the details of our lives unless we can trust the fact that what we share in the group stays in the group. Unfortunately, that is easier said than done. As Benjamin Franklin cynically remarked, "Three may keep a secret, if two of them are dead."[1] Although the rest of the body slows down with the passage of time, the tongue never seems to lose its steam, as the following anonymous verse points out:

> Our vigor wanes with middle age,
> We find our footsteps lagging;
> Our backbones creak,
> Our sight grows weak,
> And yet our tongues keep wagging.

In light of our propensity to tell — instead of keep — secrets, it comes as no surprise that Scripture has quite a bit to say on the subject of a "runaway tongue." In the Book of Proverbs we read:

> "He who holds his tongue is wise"
> (Prov. 10:19, NIV).
> "He who guards his mouth and his tongue keeps
> himself from calamity" (Prov. 21:23, NIV).
> "A gossip betrays a confidence, but a trustworthy
> person keeps a secret" (Prov. 11:13, NIV).

Moreover, in the Gospel of Mark we read of the devastating effect a betrayed confidence had on the ministry of Jesus. Jesus healed a man of leprosy, then gave him a strong warning:

> "See that you don't tell this to anyone. But go, show yourself to the priest and offer the sacrifices that Moses commanded for your cleansing, as a testimony to them." Instead he went out and began to talk freely, spreading the news. As a result, Jesus could no longer enter a town openly but stayed outside in lonely places. Yet the people still came to him from everywhere. (Mark 1:44–45, NIV)

Did you catch the effect of the broken confidence? No longer was Jesus able to enter cities or towns without great difficulty. The betrayed trust forced him to change his approach to ministry and stay on the periphery of population centers. He could no longer easily enter metropolitan areas. Remember the old children's ditty: "Sticks and stones may break my bones, but words will never hurt me"? That did not prove to be true in Jesus' life.

Neither does it in ours. Words carelessly said, carelessly shared, can have very painful effects.

The Apostle James described the dangers of misplaced and misspoken words in his letter to the church in Jerusalem:

> When we put bits into the mouths of horses to make them obey us, we can turn the whole animal. Or take ships as an example. Although they are so large and are driven by strong winds, they are steered by a very small rudder wherever the pilot wants to go. Likewise the tongue is a small part of the body, but it makes great boasts. Consider that a great forest is set on fire by a small spark. The tongue also is a fire, a world of evil among the parts of the body. It corrupts the whole person, sets the whole course of his life on fire, and is itself set on fire by hell.
>
> All kinds of animals, birds, reptiles and creatures of the sea are being tamed and have been tamed by man, but no man can tame the tongue. It is a restless evil, full of deadly poison.
>
> With the tongue we praise our Lord and Father, and with it we curse men, who have been made in God's likeness. Out of the same mouth come praise and cursing. My brothers, this should not be. Can both fresh water and salt flow from the same spring? My brothers, can a fig tree bear olives, or a grapevine bear figs? Neither can a salt spring produce fresh water. (James 3:3–12, NIV)

The Tongue

The tongue — what a study in contrasts! What a mixture of good and bad! It praises the Lord and curses people made in God's image. With it we encourage our children, comfort our friends, communicate our thoughts, defend the truth, and confess our sins. Yet we also use it to break promises, gossip, and destroy. This dark side of the tongue did not go unnoticed by James. In fact, he stressed it in great detail to make us aware of its dangers.

He likened it to a tiny flame that sets off a forest fire. James' fiery picture brings back vivid memories of my high school days in Glendale, California. The climate and vegetation in Southern California are quite similar to the tinder-dry wood and scrub of Palestine with which James was familiar. It does not take much in such a climate to start a ravaging fire, and almost every summer fires rage out of control in the Los Angeles mountains. One particular summer remains vivid in my mind. It was my junior year in high school. A fire in the adjacent Verdugo Mountains rolled down a mountain canyon, threatening the home of my good friend Lee Shalhoub. I recall standing on the roof of Lee's house, hose in hand, watering down his shake-shingle roof so that nearby sparks would not set fire to his home. Fortunately, the wind changed and Lee's home was spared.

Fires in Southern California — fires in Palestine — start easily and burn rapidly. This is the picture James paints of the tongue. He describes it as a spark that can set off a damaging fire. He paints a picture of a handful of words that can destroy a relationship or reputation.

William Barclay, reflecting on James' word picture, said there are two ways the tongue is like a forest fire. One, it is wide-ranging and can damage at a distance. A chance word dropped in one place can quickly spread to another. A person can drop a word or story about someone a hundred miles away and that word can cause infinite damage and harm if spoken inappropriately.

Secondly, Barclay says, the tongue is like a forest fire because it is quite uncontrollable. Once a word is spoken, there is no getting it back. "Three things come not back — the spent arrow, the spoken word and the lost opportunity." Therefore, Barclay counsels, "Let a person, before he speaks, remember that once a word is spoken it is gone from his control; and let him think before he speaks, because, although he cannot get it back, he will most certainly answer for it."[2]

Maybe you recall what carelessly spoken words did to the grave of Abraham Lincoln. Twice his coffin was re-opened. The first time was 1887, twenty-two years after his assassination. Rumors were spreading like wildfire that his coffin was empty, so it was re-opened in order for a select group of witnesses to set the record straight. The rumor proved false. Fourteen years later, though, the coffin was re-opened again. Why? The same rumors spread like a prairie-fire once again. This time, over the protests of Lincoln's son Robert, an even larger group of witnesses pried open the casket to see for themselves. The rumors again proved false, and after this episode the corpse was permanently embedded in a crypt in Springfield, Illinois.

What comes out of our mouths can singe and sear, devastate and destroy. According to James, the tongue can be volatile as well as vital, and nowhere is that more evident than when people count on us to keep quiet, to keep their confidences. When we maintain confidentiality — keep in the group what we share — the group becomes vital, a place where we can indeed bare our burdens. For we know they will not be spread elsewhere. We feel free to share things we never thought possible, for we know these people can be trusted with the intimate details of our lives. However, if that trust is broken, if what we share goes outside the group, then we will retreat, and probably even leave, unless confidentiality is restored. When promises are broken and trust is betrayed, we become hurt and angry. What was once vital becomes volatile. When confidentiality is broken the group is in grave danger, facing potentially explosive destruction, unless something is done about the breakdown of trust. Simply put, "If I cannot trust you with the details of my life, then I will stop sharing them with you, and in all likelihood I will go somewhere where people will keep what I share to themselves."

Broken Confidences

In his book *Covenant to Care*, Louis Evans Jr. offers wise counsel about the breakdown of confidentiality in small groups:

> One way to shut down a group very quickly is to break the covenant of confidentiality. If someone breaks that confidence, then in all love and honesty he or she must be encountered. In so doing, it may become apparent why this person needs to share

such information outside the group, and that in itself can be therapeutic. Until the leak is stopped, the group will have little sense of freedom, and the others in covenant will find tough going with their little ship of covenant relationships floundering because of the weight of mistrust that seeped into the process through such a leak.[3]

Such an encounter happened recently in our congregation. A person in one of our small groups, thinking he would help another member, told one of our pastoral staff about an automobile accident the member's daughter had had recently. When the staff person saw the member the next week he said, "Tell me about your daughter's recent accident, and how can I be praying for you and her?"

It was an innocent, pastoral request, but the woman was livid because no one was supposed to know about the accident except the members of her small group. At the next meeting she shared her anger about the broken confidence and wondered who did it. The member who had revealed the information confessed, "It was me. I was only trying to help. I was not thinking. I should have been more careful. Will you forgive me?"

The woman said, "Yes I will forgive you, but let's talk about confidentiality a little bit. When I speak of confidentiality, I understand that to mean whatever is shared in the group stays in the group — unless I am suicidal or homicidal. Unless I am thinking of hurting myself physically or someone else physically, everything I share with you stays here in the group. Is that our understanding of what it means to uphold confidentiality in our group?"

The group talked about confidentiality and finally agreed upon her definition — no breaking of confidentiality unless someone was suicidal or homicidal; that is, unless someone was contemplating harming themself or someone else. Then the proper helping professionals or authorities would need to be notified. Everything else, though, would stay in the group unless prior permission was given to share the information outside.

The good news in all this is that the breakdown was faced immediately and the group used it to define specifically what they meant by confidentiality, keeping them together for years to come. They successfully diffused the volatile situation caused by an errant tongue.

Of course, we wish all breakdowns in confidentiality had such a storybook ending. However, we know they do not. Sometimes the damage is too great. Many times it takes considerable time to learn how to trust again. Moreover, every now and again, as a result of a betrayed confidence, a person will drop out of a small group without saying why. In light of such damage, this portion of the Hippocratic Oath should apply not only to physicians but also to small group members:

> And whatsoever I shall see or hear in the course of my profession [substitute "in my small group"] . . . if it be what should not be published abroad, I will never divulge, holding such things to be holy secrets.

Holy Ground

When someone shares with us the intimate details of his or her life, we are on holy ground. When they allow us to help bear one of their burdens, we are given a sacred trust. Moreover, when trusted with the raw material of someone's life, we have been enormously affirmed. We have been told, "I trust you. I can count on you. I believe in you." Few gifts rival the gift of trust.

Painfully, I recall one of the times I abused the gift. It was not intentional, but that does not excuse me. It happened with a member of my family. I shared an incident about my daughter in a sermon without checking with her first. It made for a funny sermon illustration, but my daughter was bothered and hurt that everyone in the church knew what she had done. I felt terrible, asked her forgiveness, and we worked out a mutually agreeable arrangement. If I was going to mention her or her brother by name in a sermon, I would check with them first and pay them one dollar for the use of their name. If they did not approve of their story being told, I would not use it in the sermon. The system continues to work well; however, I wish my daughter's trust, for a period of time, had not been the system's price tag.

On a windswept hill in an English church graveyard stands a weatherbeaten tombstone. It reads:

Beneath this stone, a Lump of Clay,
Lies Arabella Young,
Who, on this 24th of May,
Began to Hold Her Tongue!

May we learn how to do that now instead of later, because upon the foundation of confidentiality is built the freedom to express one's personal thoughts, feelings, and beliefs. Confidentiality is the back-bone of every small group. A group without it quickly deteriorates. Simply put:

*The extent to which we can trust others
is the extent to which we allow them into our lives.
We can hardly bear one another's burdens
if they cannot trust their burdens to us.*

STUDY SIX
Bearing One Another's Burdens (Confidentiality)

1. **Check-In** *(30–40 minutes)*
    Complete the following sentences:

    - "As a child the person to whom I told my secrets was ..."
    - "If someone were to betray a confidence of mine, I would probably ..."
    - "Something I want to tell you about my week, trusting you will keep it to yourself, is ..."

2. **Study** *(20 minutes)*
    Discuss the reading. What surprised you? Challenged you? Comforted you? Bothered you?

If you are the enabler leading the discussion, strive for an atmosphere of openness and inclusiveness. Attempt to include everyone in the discussion and stress that there is no such thing as a "stupid question."

There are three discussion skills that are very important. One is *Information and Opinion Seeking*. This skill can be used to involve those who have not spoken in the group or whose ideas or opinions should be brought into the discussion. Two examples of information and opinion seeking are:

"John, what do you think?"
"Mary, I would be interested in your opinion."

Often during discussion times a handful of group members fail to participate. Seeking their opinions tells each group member that their thoughts and ideas are valued.

Another discussion skill is *Extending*. This involves building on the discussion thought line. After someone gives an answer or makes a comment, extending remarks include:

"Does anyone have anything to add to what has been said?"
"Have we left out anything important?"
"Is there anything else that comes to mind?"

A third small group discussion skill is *Clarification*. During a group discussion, comments may be made that are not fully understood by a listener. We often assume we know what is being said, but in reality we are making a guess. The result is misunderstanding and vagueness. Typical clarification comments are:

"Could you restate that?"
"Do you mean to say...?"
"What I heard you say is.... Is that correct?"

Clarifying what group members are saying tells them we are interested in understanding them. Remember, communication exists only when it is understood in the same sense the speaker meant it.

Define how you see confidentiality operating in your group. Which of the following comes closest to describing your understanding of confidentiality?

- "I trust your judgment. If you think it would help me if someone outside the group knew about a certain

situation in my life, feel free to share it with them. However, ask those individuals to keep it to themselves."
- "What is said in the group stays in the group."
- "I will tell you what is confidential and what is not. If I do not tell you something is confidential, feel free to share it outside the group."

Determine your preferred way of dealing with a breakdown in confidentiality. Do you prefer to deal with it one-on-one with the person involved or as a group?

3. **Prayer Concerns** *(30–45 minutes)*
    Share your prayer requests.

4. **Prayer** *(10–15 minutes)*
    Close your group in prayer. (Refer back to Chapter Three for some different ways this might be done.)

5. **Assignment**
    Assign Chapter 7 for next week's reading.

CHAPTER 7

Encourage and Build Up One Another

Therefore encourage one another
and build each other up,
just as in fact you are doing.

I Thessalonians 5:11 (NIV)

A few years ago my Tuesday night small group studied *The Passionate People* by Bruce Larson and Keith Miller.[1] Of all the things addressed in the book, one concept has stayed with me to this day. It is Keith Miller's description of "balcony people" in contrast to "basement people." According to Miller, the followers of Sigmund Freud support the theory that we are all controlled to some extent by basement people. These are people from our past (e.g., parents, school teachers, and others) who go with us everywhere, reach into our unconscious and drag us down. Freudians see these basement people as negative influences in our lives and claim the overwhelming majority of us are filled with basement people messages like:

> "You can't do that."
> "That's a stupid thing to do."
> "When are you ever going to get it right?"

Lucy, of the Peanuts Gang, is a classic basement person:

Basement people divert (or try to divert) us from our hopes and dreams. They constantly point out what is wrong, rather than what is right with us. They stress the negative, rather than the positive. Basement people cause a room to light up when they leave.

Miller also describes "balcony people." They are people who are full of love, who cheer us on to be loving, courageous, and risky saints when we are tempted to give up. They sit in the balcony of our lives like a heavenly cheering section, saying, "You can do it! Remember how you handled this before! You can make it! Go for the brass ring!"

Balcony People

Balcony people are the great encouragers in our lives. They are the kind of people who helped the renowned therapist Carl Rogers become all he could be. In a speech in 1964, he said:

> When I am not prized or appreciated, I do not only feel very much diminished, I am greatly diminished in my behavior. When I am prized, I blossom. I expand, I am an interesting individual. In a group which is hostile or unappreciative I am just not much of anything. People wonder with very good reason, how did he ever get a reputation? I wish I had the strength to be somewhat more similar in both kinds of groups, but actually the person I am in a warm and interested group is very different from the person I am in a hostile or a cold group.

A balcony person enabled Robert Manry to fulfill a lifelong dream. Charles Swindoll tells Manry's story in his book *The Quest for Character.*[2] After ten years of faithful desk work as a copywriter for the *Cleveland Plain Dealer*, Manry took a leave of absence to fulfill his dream of sailing alone from Falmouth, Massachusetts, to Falmouth, England. If successful, his would be the smallest craft ever to make the voyage.

Manry, however, did not share his dream with many people — he was afraid they would try to dissuade him. But when he told his wife, Virginia, his wild idea, she said, "Go for it!"

So, on May 24, 1965, Manry and his thirteen-and-a-half-foot boat slipped out of a Massachusetts marina headed for

England. Seventy-eight days later, as he finally neared the British coast, he hoped to interest someone in buying the rights to his story and so offset the cost of his adventure. When he arrived, however, he could not believe his eyes — forty thousand people were there cheering him on! In front was Virginia, who had refused to be rigid, closed, or negative as his dream took shape.

Scripture calls us to be balcony people. Granted, not in those words — the exact command is "Encourage one another and build each other up" (I Thess. 5:11, NIV). If ever there was a balcony person in Scripture, it was the man named Barnabas. We meet him in the Book of Acts, where he vouched for Paul to the apostles.

Paul, being persona non grata in Damascus where the Jews had conspired to kill him, traveled to Jerusalem to join the disciples and was surprised at their cool, suspicious reception.

> When he came to Jerusalem, he tried to join the disciples, but they were all afraid of him, not believing that he really was a disciple. But Barnabas took him and brought him to the apostles. He told them how Saul on this journey had seen the Lord and that the Lord had spoken to him and how in Damascus he had preached fearlessly in the name of Jesus. So Saul stayed with them and moved about freely in Jerusalem, speaking boldly in the name of the Lord. He talked and debated with the Grecian Jews, but they tried to kill him. When the brothers learned of this, they took him down to Caesarea and sent him off to Tarsus.
>
> Then the church throughout Judea, Galilee, and Samaria enjoyed a time of peace. It was strengthened; and encouraged by the Holy Spirit, it grew in numbers, living in the fear of the Lord. (Acts 9:26-31, NIV)

Though Paul was accepted by the church in Damascus, many Jerusalem Christians remembered how he had treated Stephen and would not forgive him. Others thought him a wolf in sheep's clothing, pretending to be a Christian only to betray all the

Christians in Jerusalem to Jewish authorities. In short, most disciples in Jerusalem doubted he was one of them. But not Barnabas. Luke introduced Barnabas with the words, "Barnabas (which means Son of Encouragement)" (Acts 4:36, NIV).

Barnabas came to Paul's rescue, sponsoring him before Peter and James, the influential apostles in Jerusalem. He asked them to acknowledge Paul as a fellow apostle. Barnabas became a balcony person by saying in effect to Peter and James, "He can do it! He's for real! Give him a chance!" On the strength of this recommendation, Peter and James did just that and the rest is history — as Paul eventually became the Apostle to the Gentiles.

Throughout Acts we meet Barnabas again and again, always helping, encouraging, and uplifting others. Ten years after the Jerusalem incident he would travel to Tarsus to take Paul with him on a missionary journey. Two years later he would stand up for a young man named Mark, who would eventually write one of the four gospels. Mark was a young missionary drop-out whom Paul wanted to send home, but Barnabas would have none of it. Instead, Barnabas took him on a missionary journey, while Paul took Silas. Barnabas' ministry with Paul, his belief in Mark, his faithfulness when Paul was imprisoned, and his consistency in helping new Christians gave him the designation "Son of Encouragement" in the early church.

Years later Paul wrote to the Thessalonians, inviting them — and us — to be like Barnabas: "Encourage one another and build each other up" (I Thess. 5:11, NIV). What would it be like for us to join "The Order of Barnabas"? It would require adopting the following five mottoes.

Mottoes of the Order of Barnabas

1. Be vocal in the affirmation of others.

Some years ago I heard of a twelve-year-old boy who could not talk. After being served oatmeal for several days in a row, however, he amazingly blurted out, "Yuck! I hate oatmeal."

His mother was overwhelmed. She ran across the room, threw her arms around his neck and cried, "For twelve long years your father and I were convinced you couldn't talk. Why have you never spoken to us?"

Bluntly, he explained, "Up until now everything has been okay!"

For some strange reason, many of us are like that boy. We are stingy in our praise. Yet, sharing affirmation is so important in helping others grow. Too often we take the attitude of the peasant woman in *Fiddler on the Roof*. When asked by her husband if she loved him, she replied that she had cleaned and cooked for him for twenty-five years — why speak of love now?

Why? As Carl Rogers said earlier, "When I am prized I blossom, I expand, I am an interesting individual." Members of The Order of Barnabas help others blossom by watering their lives with vocal affirmation.

2. Affirm people for who they are, not who you want them to be.

I am a sports fan, and when my son Josh was born, I had a lot of expectations. I hoped he would love sports as much as I. I looked forward to days as a Little League coach, with him as the star of the team. I could hardly wait to watch him score the winning touchdown against his cross-town high school rival.

But Josh did not share my enthusiasm for those things. He played one year of T-ball and put away his baseball glove. He ran one year of track and hung up his spikes. And he never tried out for the football team. Instead, his interest as a little boy gravitated to building blocks and Legos™, and as an adolescent, to computers and cars.

Am I disappointed? No. In fact, just the opposite is true. I am as proud of him as a parent could be. I do not recall when and where it happened, but someone advised me as a young parent to affirm my children for who they were rather than who I wanted them to be. I tried to do that with Josh. I affirmed his interest in building things and discovering how things worked. I tried to do my best to understand rpm's and dual overhead cam engines. I think I succeeded. In fact, when Josh reads this book, it will probably be the first time he ever knew of my hopes for him when he was born.

I do not have those hopes any longer. Instead, I thank God for the unique gift that Josh is. Even though different from who I expected, he became as enjoyable as the person I had ever hoped for. How miserable he would have been if I had insisted on his fulfilling my dreams and expectations. Affirm people for who they are and not who we want them to be. It works not only for children, but for adults as well.

3. "Grab a crab."

A few Christmases ago my wife's parents visited us in Brookings, Oregon. Because they love shellfish, Trudy arranged with a friend at the Port of Brookings to obtain six crabs. After work we went to the port office where Trudy went in to pick them up. She returned looking troubled, and said, "Dick, they are crawlers!"

That meant they were alive and crawling around. Rather squeemishly, she asked me to put them in the car. Now that was the last thing I wanted to do! Spiders give me the creeps, let alone crabs. For that matter, I do not even like shellfish! I hate seafood! I was doing all this for my in-laws, not me. But I knew Trudy did not want to touch a crab, and I did not want to appear a wimp with all those burly fishermen nearby, so I reluctantly said, "Okay," found out from a guy on the dock how to pick up crabs without losing a finger, and put them in the trunk of our car.

The point is, members of The Order of Barnabas have this incredible knack of "grabbing crabs." They can encourage and affirm the most disagreeable, critical, and unloving sorts of people. Maybe it is a boss giving us fits, a neighbor driving us up a wall, or a relative we suspect got switched in the hospital nursery. Whoever they are, there is something about them that can be affirmed. Members of The Order of Barnabas look for such things, point them out, and spur individuals on to be all that they can be.

4. Be a rainbow, not a cloudburst.

People in The Order of Barnabas do not rain on other people's parades. Rather, they hold up people's unlimited possibilities. Bishop Fulton Sheen once related a conversation he had had with a woman in the elevator of a department store. He was shopping on the fifth floor and wanted to go to the sixth. So he stepped on the elevator with a few other passengers. Just as the elevator operator said, "Going up!" a woman rushed out madly saying, "I don't want to go up. I want to go down." Noticing Sheen's clerical collar, she turned to him and said, "I didn't think I could go wrong following you!"

He replied, "Madam, I only take people up, not down."[3]

That is what members of The Order of Barnabas do. They look for ways to build people up, not tear them down.

5. Allow others to be your balcony people.

This may be the most difficult part of The Order. It often is easier to give encouragement than to receive it. I think of my secretary, Marge Tilton. In staff meeting one day we were discussing the importance of accepting and believing the good things people say about us. As we talked, Denn Denning, one of our pastoral staff, said, "Marge, you are so warm and friendly to people when they call."

Marge replied, "That is because I grew up in a small town and my father was friendly."

I loved Denn's response. He said, "Marge, a number of people grow up in small towns with friendly fathers, and they are not nearly as warm and friendly and outgoing as you. Will you accept that affirmation for yourself?"

When Corrie Ten Boom, author of *The Hiding Place*, was complimented or affirmed she always would say, "Thank you," likening each affirmation to a pretty flower. At the end of the day she gathered her flowers of affirmation into a bouquet and gave them to Christ, and thanked Him for loving her and making her so special.

We are special. We are gifted. We are worthy of affirmation. When someone affirms us, may we accept it and thank God for making us so unique.

Perhaps this "Froghood" parable written by Wes Seeliger sums up our ministry to one another:

> Ever feel like a frog? Frogs feel slow, low, ugly, puffy, drooped, pooped. I know. One told me. The frog feeling comes when — you want to be bright, but feel dull. You want to share, but are selfish. You want to be thankful, but feel resentment. You want to be big, but are small. You want to care, but are indifferent.
>
> Yes, at one time or another each of us has found [ourselves] on a lily pad floating down the great river of life. Frightened and disgusted, but too froggish to budge.
>
> Once upon a time there was a frog. But he really wasn't a frog. He was a prince who looked and felt like a frog. A wicked witch had cast a spell on him. Only the kiss of a beautiful young maiden could save him. . . . So there he sat — an unkissed prince in frog form.
>
> But miracles happen. One day a beautiful maiden grabbed him up and gave him a big smack. Crash — Boom — Zap! There he was — a handsome prince. And you know the rest. They lived happily ever after. [4]

So what is the task of the church? TO KISS FROGS, of course.

STUDY SEVEN
Encouraging and Building Up One Another

1.   Check-In *(25–35 minutes)*

A "Big Pretty" is a time when you have felt really affirmed. A "Big Ugly" is a time when you have been hurt, put down, disaffirmed. Take three to five minutes and think about a "Big

Pretty" and a "Big Ugly" in your life, and then take turns sharing the pretty and the ugly with the group.

2.   Study *(15–20 minutes)*
Choose one thing from the chapter that was meaningful or important, and share why you chose it.

3.   Affirming One Another *(25–35 minutes)*
This exercise is taken from Lyman Coleman's *Beginnings*.[5] In the exercise you will be comparing the people in your group to nautical vessels. Here are the instructions: Jot down each person's name next to the vessel that best describes them. If possible, choose a different vessel for each person. After everyone is finished, each person sits in silence while others in the group explain why they chose a particular vessel for him or her. Then each person tells what vessel they would have picked for themselves.

Nautical Affirmation Exercise

_____	Tenacious Tug Boat
_____	Toy Sail Boat
_____	Tom Sawyer Wood Raft
_____	Cruising Yacht
_____	High-Speed Motorboat
_____	Venetian Gondola
_____	Mythical Treasure Ship
_____	Sleek Hydrofoil
_____	Mississippi River Ferry Boat
_____	Rubber Dingy
_____	Old-Fashioned Row Boat
_____	Clipper Ship
_____	Other

4. **Prayer Concerns** *(20–25 minutes)*

5. **Prayer** *(5 minutes)*

6. **Assignment**
    Assign Chapter 8 for next week's reading.

CHAPTER

Submit to ONE Another

Submit to one another
out of reverence for Christ.

Ephesians 5:21 (NIV)

J ames Dobson, founder and president of "Focus on the Family," relates a marvelous story about the difficulty we have submitting to one another:

> In the absence of parental leadership, some children become extremely obnoxious and defiant, especially in public places. Perhaps the best example was a ten-year-old boy named Robert, who was a patient of my good friend, Dr. William Slonecker. Dr. Slonecker said his pediatric staff dreaded the days when Robert was scheduled for an office visit. He literally attacked the clinic, grabbing instruments and files and telephones. His passive mother could do little more than shake her head in bewilderment.
>
> During one physical examination, Dr. Slonecker observed severe cavities in Robert's teeth and knew that the boy must be referred to a local dentist. But who would be given the honor? A referral like Robert could mean the end of a professional friendship. Dr. Slonecker eventually decided to send him to an older dentist who reportedly understood children. The confrontation that followed now stands as one of the classic moments in the history of human conflict.
>
> Robert arrived in the dental office, prepared for battle.
>
> "Get in the chair, young man," said the doctor.
>
> "No chance!" replied the boy.
>
> "Son, I told you to climb onto the chair, and that's what I intend for you to do," said the dentist.
>
> Robert stared at his opponent for a moment and then replied, "If you make me get in that chair, I will take off all my clothes."
>
> The dentist calmly said, "Son, take them off."
>
> The boy forthwith removed his shirt, undershirt, shoes and socks, and then looked up in defiance.
>
> "All right, son," said the dentist. "Now get in the chair."

"You didn't hear me," sputtered Robert. "I said if you make me get on that chair, I will take off all my clothes."

"Son, take them off," replied the man.

Robert proceeded to remove his pants and shorts, finally standing totally naked before the dentist and his assistant.

"Now, son, get in the chair," said the doctor.

Robert did as he was told, and sat cooperatively through the entire procedure. When the cavities were drilled and filled, he was instructed to step down from the chair.

"Give me my clothes now," said the boy.

"I'm sorry," replied the dentist. "Tell your mother that we're going to keep your clothes tonight. She can pick them up tomorrow."

Can you comprehend the shock Robert's mother received when the door to the waiting room opened, and there stood her pink son, as naked as the day he was born? The room was filled with patients, but Robert and his mom walked past them and into the hall. They went down the public elevator and into the parking lot, ignoring the snickers of onlookers.

The next day, Robert's mother returned to retrieve his clothes, and asked to have a word with the dentist. However, she did not come to protest. These were her sentiments: "You don't know how much I appreciate what happened here yesterday. You see, Robert has been blackmailing me about his clothes for years. Whenever we are in a public place, such as a grocery store, he makes unreasonable demands of me. If I don't immediately buy him what he wants, he threatens to take off all his clothes. You are the first person who called his bluff, doctor, and the impact on Robert has been incredible.[1]

Like Robert, many of us will do whatever is necessary to get our way. In fact, that is exactly how Philip Crosby described human nature in his book *The Art of Getting Your Own Sweet Way*.

"People are not complex," he says. "They really just want to achieve their personal definition of peace and quiet and to have their own sweet way."[2]

Of course, this spills over into the church. Most church fights and splits occur because people do not want to give in to one another. Rather, they insist a critical issue is at stake. They claim they are fighting for a sacred principle. Sometimes that is true, but usually not. Often we do not give in simply because giving in would mean not getting our way. Unlike ten-year-old Robert, however, we do not threaten to take off our clothes. Maybe it would be better if we did, every time we were tempted to dig in our heels. It might help us be more discerning about what is really important and more selective when we take our stands.

Discriminating behavior is recommended in Scripture. We are encouraged, at times, to give in rather than dig in. We are commanded not to constantly push our own agenda, but to defer to the needs, desires, and wishes of others. The Apostle Paul encourages us to "Submit to one another out of reverence to Jesus Christ" (Eph. 5:21, NIV). Paul not only commands it, he models it:

> When we arrived at Jerusalem, the brothers received us warmly. The next day Paul and the rest of us went to see James, and all the elders were present. Paul greeted them and reported in detail what God had done among the Gentiles through his ministry.
>
> When they heard this, they praised God. Then they said to Paul: "You see, brother, how many thousands of Jews have believed, and all of them are zealous for the law. They have been informed that you teach all the Jews who live among the Gentiles to turn away from Moses, telling them not to circumcise their children or live according to our customs. What shall we do? They will certainly hear that you have come. (Acts 21:17–22, NIV)

This event took place after Paul's third missionary journey. Let us be clear about the problem. Rumors had spread to Jerusalem that he had encouraged Jewish Christians to forsake their ancestral faith and customs. It may be difficult for us to understand the threat this posed to some Jewish Christians. A parallel for today would be someone telling Christians in America that, "Since you believe in God, you no longer need to observe your nation's holidays. The Fourth of July and President's Day are definitely out. Also, the Constitution. They used to be helpful but now they have been replaced by something better. Don't pay attention to them."

For the Jews, their religious and national heritage were intertwined. The law was more a part of their lives than the Constitution is of ours. This did not change when Jews began following Christ. They still honored the law, observed the Passover, and circumcised male infants. So when rumors reached Jerusalem, the center of Jewish Christianity, that Paul was telling Jewish Christians to abandon their ancient customs, a problem arose. Of course, Paul never tried to draw them from away from these customs, but insisted only that Jewish law was irrelevant for the Gentile. In fact, in the previous chapter of Acts, Luke related a story of Paul's observance of Jewish custom: When Paul left Corinth, he shaved his head as part of a Nazarite vow.

Faced with this unfounded rumor, the elders suggested a solution:

> Do what we tell you. There are four men with us who have made a vow. Take these men, join in their purification rites and pay their expenses, so that they can have their heads shaved. Then everybody will know there is no truth in these reports about you, but that you yourself are living in obedience to the law. (Acts 21:23–24, NIV)

This is the same vow that Paul took when leaving Corinth. A Nazarite vow was quite involved and often was taken to thank God for some blessing. It entailed abstaining from meat and wine for thirty days. Afterward, certain offerings were made — a year-old lamb for a sin offering, a ram for a peace offering. In addition, one's hair was shorn and burned on the altar with the sacrifices. This vow was costly and beyond the resources of many. It therefore was considered an act of piety for a wealthier person to defray the expenses of someone taking the vows.

That is what Paul was asked to do: finance these four men and demonstrate that he was not opposed to Jewish Christians observing Jewish customs.

Would he do it? Paul knew there was no truth to the rumors. Why submit to this expense when he was right? Would this compromise his integrity? Why not say, "Those people are wrong and that is their problem; I am not going to do this; I am, after all, an *apostle*"?

I identify with Paul here. A few years ago, I was asked to respond to an unfounded rumor. It involved my presbytery.

I was rumored to be a "suspect Presbyterian." Some might take that as a compliment. I did not. I am thankful things have changed drastically, and I no longer hear those rumors. At one time, though, some colleagues questioned my commitment to the Presbyterian church. I see now why they might have thought such a thing. After all, I was raised Roman Catholic, graduated from a non-Presbyterian seminary, and pastor an atypical Presbyterian church. In addition, I see myself as a Christian first and a Presbyterian second. However, being rumored a "suspect Presbyterian" hurt, for I have a great love for my denomination.

When my friends in the presbytery heard the rumors, they encouraged me to do something about them. I did not have to shave my head, but I did have to make more time for presbytery functions, committee meetings, and weekly pastors' lunches. I was told that if I became more involved in presbytery, people would get to know me and see that the rumors were unfounded. I took this advice, and now very few, if any, colleagues in our presbytery see me as a "suspect Presbyterian." However, I would be less than honest if I told you I did not resent having to go that extra mile to overcome the rumor.

While I may be projecting my own experience onto the Apostle Paul, I would guess he had difficulty with the elders' request as well. In fact, William Barclay, the great New Testament scholar, said, "There can be no doubt that this matter was distasteful to Paul. So what did Paul do?"[3]

> The next day Paul took the men and purified himself along with them. Then he went to the temple to give notice of the date when the days of purification would end and the offering would be made for each of them. (Acts 21:26, NIV)

Paul submitted! Why? Luke did not say. I think it was because more than Paul's pride or ego was at stake — it was the unity of the church. He willingly set aside being right for this higher good. Paul's actions, and his subsequent encouragement to "Submit to one another out of reverence for Christ," give us much to consider about this thing called "submission."

Four Statements Concerning Submission

1. Submission fosters freedom.

What is freedom? It is the ability to lay down the burden of always needing to get our own way. Listen to Richard Foster, Professor of Theology at Friends University:

> The obsession to demand that things go the way we want them to go is one of the greatest bondages in human society today. People will spend weeks, months, and even years in a perpetual stew because some little thing did not go as they wished. They will fuss and fume. They will get mad about it. They will act as if their very life hangs on the issue. They may even get an ulcer over it.[4]

How true. At the seven-year mark in our marriage, Trudy and I had a horrendous time together. No week passed without a knock-down, drag-out battle, punctuated by periods of silence and pouting. It was not until we faced the question, "Do we want to be right or be married?" that healing came. We decided we wanted to stay married, and we agreed to lay aside our mutual desire to always be right. We no longer had to win every argument, and our marriage turned around. We were free to love one another again. Submission fosters freedom. Our marriage has grown since that turbulent year in direct proportion to our ability to practice mutual submission.

2. Submission is a clear call to all Christians.

Martin Luther said, "A Christian . . . is the most free lord of all and subject to no one; a Christian . . . is the most dutiful servant to all and subject to everyone."

We cannot read the New Testament without coming across the call to lay aside our desires — at times — for the good of Christ and one another. Paul enjoins us, "Submit to one another out of reverence for Christ" (Eph. 5:21, NIV). Jesus states, "If anyone would come after me, he must deny himself and take up his cross and follow me" (Mark 8:34, NIV). Paul comments, "To those under the law, I become as one under the law . . . so as to win those under the law" (I Cor. 9:20, NIV).

3. Submission brings joy.

Great joy can be found in submission, though we often do not think so. We think joy comes in self-actualization, and at times it does. But it also comes in acts of self-denial. Surrendering our rights for the needs of others can have an amazingly positive effect upon us. I think of the story of the Iron Cross. During his reign, King Frederick William III of Prussia found himself in trouble. His wars had been costly, and he was seriously short of finances. He could not disappoint his people, and capitulation to the enemy was unthinkable.

After careful reflection he asked the women of Prussia to bring their gold and silver jewelry to be melted down for the country. For each article received, he exchanged a cross of iron as a symbol of his gratitude. Each was inscribed "I gave gold for iron, 1813."

The response was overwhelming. These women prized their gifts from the king more highly than their former jewelry. The reason? They experienced joy in sacrificing something for a greater cause, a higher purpose. The Iron Crosses symbolized that joy.

4. Submission requires prayer and discernment.

Someone once described parenting as "the art of knowing when to hold on and when to let go." A popular song has described the game of poker as the art of knowing when to "hold" the cards and when to "fold" them. This applies to the art of submission. How do we know when to "hold them" and when to "fold them"? How do we know when to hold on and when to let go?

To always hold on to the position of being right would make us unpleasantly rigid. To always give in would make us spineless saps. To know when to give in and when to dig in is not easy. Like most biblical commands, the injunction to submit to one another does not give us specific, once-and-for-all directions. Only when we know the heart of the one who lived the cross life will we develop our abilities to discern stubbornness from strength, weakness from submission.

Submission and Small Groups

Part of coming to terms with submission and small group life is the need to dispel two particular mindsets. First, is the dream of joining the "perfect" small group. There is no such thing. When we think of the perfect group, we usually envision one as *we* would like it. For me, everyone would always be on time, everyone would study the kinds of books I like, and we would make better use of our prayer time. (I sometimes become very bored when we pray at length.)

The trouble is, there is no such thing as a perfect group. Even Christ's small group was imperfect, as evidenced by constant back-biting, Judas Iscariot's betrayal, and their subsequent breakup. When we live in submission with one another, we will not get everything we want. There will be trade-offs because we all have different needs and ways of doing things. When two people gather, the possibility of the "perfect" group goes out the window. What is perfect for one will not be perfect for someone else. Instead, we need to focus on being the *best* group we can be, considering the needs and desires of ourselves *and* others.

The second misleading mindset involves accountability. Often people withhold their sharing because they are not sure they want to be held accountable for doing anything about it.

Are we willing to say to one another, "Here is who I am; this is what I want to do; hold me accountable for it"? Are we willing to submit ourself to the other members of the group in that way? Louis Evans Jr. states:

> The purpose of the covenant of accountability is to stimulate a person to grow and to come to grips with the true nature of the problems of life, accepting the resources available for liberation. Moreover, the covenant of accountability encourages the person to stay in the encounter, continue the engagement, and resist quitting when the work is only half done. It helps the person work out the plan.[5]

Lloyd Ogilvie, in his devotional work *God's Best for My Life,* suggests three steps we must take if we desire change: "Admit, Submit, Commit."[6] Are we willing to admit where we need to grow, submit ourselves to the group by requesting their help, and commit to doing something about it?

STUDY EIGHT
Submitting to One Another

1. **Check-In** *(20–30 minutes)*

   - Where did you "dig in" this week (or recently), insisting on your way?
   - Where did you "give in," doing what someone else wanted to do?

2. **Exploration** *(30–40 minutes)*

   Discuss the chapter. What struck you? Challenged you? Offended you? Confused you? Excited you?

Take a few minutes of silence to jot on a piece of paper three things you would like to see your group continue, start, or do better. It might be to:

- continue the amount of time we give to our study
- cut study time in half
- pray more
- begin and end on time
- meet in different places
- meet in one central location
- do a better job of listening to each other
- not be so time-oriented
- share more deeply

What three things would make the group a better place for you?

After you have written your three things, take turns sharing them with one another. Of the three, which might you forego? Which might you hold on to? What feelings do you have as you think of submitting your desires to the needs of the group? Share those thoughts and feelings with one another.

3. **Prayer Concerns** *(30–40 minutes)*

Share your prayer requests. During this time, also share your experience with the thirty-day prayer experiment (from Chapter 3). How did upholding a group member in prayer for the thirty days impact your spiritual life and your relationship with the person for whom you were praying?

4. **Prayer** *(10 minutes)*

5. **Assignment**

Assign Chapter 9 for next week's reading.

9

Admonish

One Another

Let the word of Christ
dwell in you richly,
teach and admonish one another
in all wisdom,
and sing psalms and hymns
and spiritual songs
with thankfulness
in your hearts to God.

Colossians 3:16 (RSV)

A customer sat down at a table in a smart restaurant and tied a napkin around his neck. The manager called the waiter aside and said, "Try to make that man understand, as tactfully as possible, that the way he is wearing his napkin is not done here."

The waiter approached the customer and said, "Shave or a haircut, sir?"

Being confrontive is risky business. Most of us do not like to do it. I know I would prefer to avoid it. I enjoy being liked, and sometimes confronting makes me the "bad" guy. I also run the risk of a relationship disintegrating. The other person may get hurt or angry, and who knows what the confrontation will do to our relationship. It might improve, but it could fall apart as well. I also like harmony, and dealing with personal conflicts seems so discordant.

The biblical mandate to confront one another makes me uncomfortable. The Apostle Paul encouraged the early church to "Admonish one another with all wisdom" (Col. 3:16, RSV). I looked up the words "admonish" and "admonition" in *Webster's New World Dictionary*. They both deal with gentle warnings or reproofs. "Admonish" means to express warning about or disapproval of, especially gently, earnestly and solicitously. "Admonition" is a "gentle or friendly reproof" or "counsel or warning against fault or oversight."[1]

In other words, Paul instructs us to confront one another gently and lovingly, whenever we see someone heading in the wrong direction. A healthy small group makes room not only for encouragement and affirmation, but admonition as well.

Most of us prefer the first two responses, not the last. It is much easier to be on the giving and receiving end of encouragement and affirmation, than of admonishment. Yet all are part and parcel of healthy small group life. Unfortunately, confrontation is not something that most small groups do very well. I think of M. Scott Peck's observation of small group life in the church today. He claims that most of what we have in the church is "pseudo-community":

> The first response of a group in seeking to form
> a community is most often to try to fake it. The

members attempt to be an instant community by being extremely pleasant with one another and avoiding all disagreement. This attempt — this pretense of community — is what I term "pseudocommunity." It never works ...

In pseudocommunity a group attempts to purchase community cheaply by pretense. It is not an evil, conscious pretense of deliberate black lies. Rather, it is an unconscious, gentle process whereby people who want to be loving attempt to do so by telling little white lies, by withholding some of the truth about themselves and their feelings in order to avoid conflict. But it is still a pretense. It is an inviting but illegitimate shortcut to nowhere.

The essential dynamic of pseudocommunity is conflict-avoidance. The absence of conflict in a group is not by itself diagnostic. Genuine communities may experience lovely and sometimes lengthy periods free from conflict. But that is because they have learned how to deal with conflict rather than avoid it. Pseudocommunity is conflict-avoiding; true community is conflict-resolving.[2]

Although most of us like to avoid a conflict or hassle, we cannot for two reasons. One, love demands that we not let anyone get away with anything. We need to hold each other accountable to tell the truth about ourselves. Two, love demands that we recognize the uniqueness of others. Differences generate conflict, but conflict is neither right nor wrong — it is simply a fact of life. What matters is how we deal with the conflict.

Remember, Jesus did not avoid conflict. He lovingly confronted the rich young ruler, saying, "Go, sell what you have and give it to the poor" (Mark 10:21, RSV). He loved the young man too much to let him avoid the one thing that would meet his need, though such a confrontation was hard. We are told that when the young man heard Jesus' words, his "countenance fell and he went away sorrowful; for he had great possessions" (Mark 10:22, RSV). Jesus also confronted those who sold pigeons in the Temple, saying, "It is written, 'My house shall be called a house of prayer;

but you make it a den of robbers'" (Matt. 21:16, RSV). The Apostle Paul followed Jesus' example. In a letter to the Galatians he wrote, "When Cephas came to Antioch I opposed him to his face" (Gal. 2:11, RSV). He also confronted Peter nose-to-nose about behavior unbecoming to him and the Body of Christ.

Most of us fear confrontation because it appears so "un-Christian" or because we believe we simply have not been given permission to do so in the church. We think that conflict or disagreement is a sign of failure. If we were "holier," we would not have contentions. So we pretend they are not there, or we avoid the conflicts so we do not need to expose our failures and short-comings to others. Yet, the stalwarts of faith — Jesus himself, and Moses, Esther, Peter, Paul, John — all lived and dealt with conflict. Conflict is not a sin, but how we handle it might be.

You probably are experiencing it in your group right now. In every "normal" small group, someone does something that begins to grate on other members. You might have difficulty with someone's commitment level, or the way others interpret Scripture, or how certain individuals dominate the group. If you are a normal small group, conflict is present. What you do with it is the key. The Apostle Paul calls us to deal with it face to face, admonishing one another with all wisdom. What are you going to do with the conflicts and disagreements in your group?

Suggestion One:

Begin by reflecting
on the positive aspects
of conflict.

Not all conflict is bad. There are positive aspects to it. Consider the following:

1. Conflict protects us from blind conformity.

Martin Bolt and David Myers put it well in their book *The Human Connection*, as they describe how we usually view conflict in the church:

We believe that only a church free of conflict can provide a strong and vital witness to the world. We view even quiet dissent and disagreement as disruptive, and open conflict as destructive, as though it might shake stability and endanger the very existence of the church. Ironically, in our press for unity within the church, we may lose the very strength and vitality we seek — the vigor that healthy and loving conflict can bring.

Unthinking compliance in the church may therefore have its basis not in apathy or laziness, but in fear of conflict. The problem is that in our desire for consensus we easily fall into blind conformity. We do not openly examine doubts about whether present doctrine and practice are consistent with the Word of God.[3]

2. Conflict keeps things from getting boring.

A good argument gets the juices flowing. It causes us to think and grapple with ideas and individuals. It is not always enjoyable, but it is never boring.

3. Conflict dealt with openly and honestly can be an indicator of love and trust.

The person I confront the most is my wife, Trudy. I also am her number one protagonist. Why? Because we have established a level of love and trust our relationship, we are free to confront. We can argue because we feel secure in our relationship, and our love can take it (at least most of the time).

I find the opposite is true in other relationships in my life. When a level of love and trust has not been established, I am hesitant to argue or confront. I am not sure the relationships can sustain the conflict.

4. Conflict can move us into a deeper level of intimacy.

This is illustrated in a story related by an unnamed friend of author/priest Morton Kelsey:

My sister and I shared a painful silence that expanded to fill the whole Datsun as we drove home to the suburbs from Chicago. Without meaning to, we had reactivated old wounds and started replaying old memory tapes. The feeling of sibling rivalry had been sparked off by an incident at a downtown restaurant. Being the more extroverted of the pair, I had dominated the conversation. Beginning to pick up on the non-verbal signals sent my way by the three other group members, I realized too late that once again I had easily slid into being the center of attention, leaving my younger sister to feel dull and unexciting by comparison. How well I knew her feeling, having fumbled my way through dinner parties where everyone's verbal brilliance had left me feeling particularly undazzling.

Haltingly we began to explore our moods of hostility and resentment toward each other. "You always take over; you're always the star of the show."

I listened to her barrage of accusations, trying to understand her feelings without losing touch with the validity of my own: "I'm a natural extrovert; I'm not *trying* to outdo you."

Slowly the accusations died down and the hurt little girl feelings emerged. It was not an easy fifteen miles as we sought really to hear each other, to say to each other that we cared enough about being sisters to bother dredging up the sludge that seems to settle into familiar relationships.

What we discovered was that on the other side of the painful exploration we made was a deeper relatedness and love that we could never have touched if we had subscribed to the belief that love is without conflict.[4]

5. Dealing openly with conflict is therapeutic.

Sometimes we get mad and must do something about it. If not, blood pressures rise and stomachs tie in knots. Dealing with conflict in a group helps us to release that anger. If we deal with it right away, it does not build up, and we retain control.

Suggestion Two:

Be clear
about the goal
of confrontation.

The goal of confrontation or admonishment is to share the truth in love and to keep one another on track. Confrontation brings attention to a debilitating behavior and opens the way to change.

Paul gives an example of this in a confrontational letter he wrote to the Corinthians. They had done something unbecoming to them, detracting from the cause of Christ. Paul, out of love for them, pointed out where they had gone wrong, in order to help them be all they could be. Reflecting upon the effect of the letter, he said:

> Even if I caused you sorrow by my letter, I do not regret it. Though I did regret it — I see that my letter hurt you, but only for a little while — yet now I am happy, not because you were made sorry, but because your sorrow led you to repentance. For you became sorrowful as God intended and so were not harmed in any way by us. Godly sorrow brings repentance that leads to salvation and leaves no regret, but worldly sorrow brings death. (II Cor. 7:8–10, NIV)

Note from Paul's words how confrontation or admonishment differs from criticism. Criticism often tears down, whereas confrontation is meant to get a person back on track.

Given the intent of confrontation or admonishment, a better word for them might be David Augsburger's term "carefronting."[5] Because we care about one another, sometimes we are called upon to share tough love with each other — which may be hard at the time, but will help all of us grow to our full potential.

Suggestion Three:

Embrace the necessity
of admonishing one another.

Abraham Lincoln once said, correctly, "To sin by silence when they should protest makes cowards out of men." There is such a thing as the sin of silence.

When I made a decision to accept my first senior pastor position, I asked a pastoral friend of mine if he had any words of wisdom for me. He advised, "Nip things in the bud. Don't let them fester."

If only I had heeded his advice. Unfortunately, I learned the hard way. It began when a man was poisoning our small Bible study group with constant negative criticisms. They were a deadly venom, repeatedly stomping other's dreams and tearing people down. No one in the group, however, had the courage to care-front the man. Ultimately the group dissolved, as members excused themselves with, "I need to spend more time at home," or "I am going to be traveling a lot," or "I'm getting my needs met elsewhere." But the real reason was "Negative Ned."

After our group folded, he joined another. It dissolved as well. People from both groups wanted to be in another group, but not with Ned. This cycle happened once more, and, in all, thirty people were exposed to this man's atrocious behavior. Not one of them, myself included, had the courage or know-how to speak the truth to him in love. Finally, Ned was care-fronted, but much too late. We had committed the sin of silence by allowing his behavior to go unchecked. We had done Ned and ourselves a disservice by avoiding conflict.

In the end we felt sorry for him, and realized we had let him down. He wondered why people seemed to avoid him, why he had difficulty making significant friendships — and we never had the courage to tell him.

If a group does not deal with conflict or feel free to confront, the conflict will be swept under the rug — only to raise its ugly head by causing people to leave or making the group a "nice" and "phony" place to be. One of the marks of a healthy and mature group is its commitment and ability to deal with conflict openly and creatively. If it does not, the group will stagnate or die.

Suggestion Four:

**Learn how to admonish
one another.**

In the February, 1976, issue of *Faith at Work Magazine*, Ralph Osborne suggested these ground rules for confrontation in a healthy group:

> 1. Give this confrontation priority over the current agenda. There is no more urgent business than this!
> 2. Require of everyone involved in the confrontation the use of "I-Messages" only. Do not permit a blaming of the other for feelings that have been provoked. For instance, it is more accurate and more helpful to say...
> "When you laughed at my question, I became angry because I felt like a schoolkid asking a dumb question in a smart class." (factual ... no blaming)
> Than to say,
> "You made me angry when you laughed at my question! (Untrue! I am responsible for my own feelings/emotions ... blaming!)
> 3. Provide adequate feedback to those involved in the confrontation to help them:
>   a. Hear accurately what is really being said;
>   b. Express your feelings adequately and properly, without blaming the other for *causing* them;
>   c. Find a solution which is mutually acceptable and beneficial.[6]

In addition to Osborne's ground rules, I would add the following considerations. First, *do not admonish one another every time someone does something improper or short-sighted.* As Jesus instructed, before you criticize someone for the speck in their eye, examine the plank in your own (Matt. 7:3). Confrontation needs to be done with grace and proper timing.

Second, *confront after prayer, asking God for sensitivity on your part and openness from the other person.* Such prayer can be said even in the heat of the moment. You do not need to think about it overnight. As you are feeling nudged to confront during a meeting, you can silently pray, "Lord, is this right? If so, make me sensitive. Guard me from sarcasm, and help Fred to hear what I say in the spirit in which it is given."

Third, *affirm your love for the person as you confront.* An example might be, "Helen, I love you so much I do not want you to get away with your not calling your daughter. You said you would do that last week. You asked that we keep you accountable for it, but you did not do it. I'm confused with what you want the group and me to do about this. Help me out."

Confrontation may not be needed very often but, when required, it is important that we love each other enough to do so. Remember the Proverb:

> Wounds from a friend can be trusted, but an enemy
> multiplies kisses. (Prov. 27:6, NIV)

General Grant's faithful friend and chief of staff was the Galena lawyer John A. Rawlins — closer to Grant than any other during the war. Grant gave Rawlins his pledge to abstain from intoxicating liquors. When he broke it, Rawlins pleaded with great earnestness that Grant refrain from strong drink, for his own sake, and the nation's great and holy cause.

Faithful were the "wounds" of that friend. There stands today, in front of the Capitol in Washington, a magnificent monument to General Grant, on his horse in characteristic pose and flanked on either side by stirring battle scenes. At the other end and a little to the south of Pennsylvania Avenue is Rawlins Park, where a very ordinary statue of Grant's friend stands. One cannot help but think of this other monument when looking at Grant's grand memorial. It was Rawlins, the faithful friend, who kept Grant on his horse.

May we be faithful friends to one another.

STUDY NINE
Admonishing One Another

1. **Check-In** *(30–35 minutes)*

    - "When I think of conflict in my home during my childhood, I think of ...
    - "The place of conflict for me this past week was ..."

2. **Exploration** *(20–30 minutes)*
    Identify two things from the chapter you would like to see the group discuss. Use this as the basis for responding and reflecting on the reading.
    If it did not surface during the discussion of the chapter, review Ralph Osborne's ground rules for confrontation in a healthy group. How do members feel about following them? What would you add or delete? How do you want to handle admonishing one another?

3. **Prayer Concerns** *(30–40 minutes)*

4. **Prayer** *(10–15 minutes)*

5. **Assignment**
    Assign Chapter 10 for next week's reading.

10

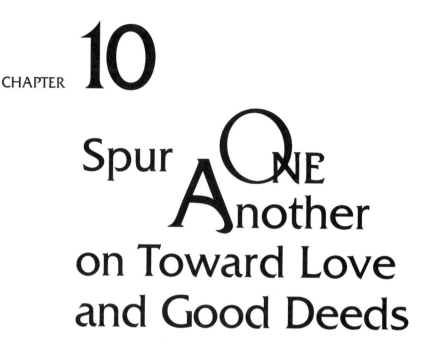

Spur ONE Another on Toward Love and Good Deeds

*And let us consider
how we may spur one another on
toward love and good deeds.*

Hebrews 10:24 (NIV)

fter preaching a six-week sermon series on the ministry of the laity, I received this note from one of our members:

Dear Dick,

It is so good to hear that as laypersons we are not second-class citizens in the church. It is good to hear that our ministry is just as important, though different, than the ministry of the clergy. For years I was led to believe that my ministry as a layperson did not measure up to that of the clergy. Thank you for the clarification and the vote of confidence.

Sincerely,
Kerry

Her note reminded me that for so long the church has overlooked and downgraded the ministry of the laity. Robert Slocum underscores this in his challenging book *Maximum Ministry.* Slocum highlights typical "church" answers to the "What next?" questions that many of us have:

. . . Finding what God has in mind for me as I prepare to be God's person in the world is not always an easy task. One reason for this difficulty is reflected in the stereotyped answer frequently given when lay men and women ask, "What's next?"

One common answer is, "Not much! After all, you're only a layperson." Of course, this answer is more often implied than spoken outright.[1]

Another message, according to Slocum, is, "Get involved in the church." (This is the answer often given by committee chairpersons in search of volunteers.) Yet, in the typical congregation, all the "church" jobs are often filled by a few members, leaving the majority to serve elsewhere.

And then there is the classic "What next?" answer usually given to the person who has a heart for God: "Go fulltime. Attend seminary and become ordained." This implies that if someone is really serious about spiritual matters they should not waste time being a layperson.

Slocum concludes:

In my own life, I have struggled with these three options — doing nothing, making my church my whole ministry, and "going professional" — and I have found all three to be unacceptable to me over the long run.[1]

Thankfully, in Scripture we find more than three options. In Scripture we discover that each of us is called to a specific ministry, and we are each uniquely gifted to accomplish that call.

Call to Ministry

From its very inception, Christianity has been a lay movement. Jesus could have called religious professionals to be part of the Twelve, but he did not. There was a plethora of scribes, rabbis, and priests, yet he chose none from their ranks. Instead, he called fishermen, tax collectors, and political activists to usher in the Kingdom of God.

In addition, the Apostle Peter calls each one of us priests: "But you are a chosen people, a royal priesthood" (I Peter 2:9, NIV). And the Apostle Paul said the major task of every pastor is to train and equip the saints for ministry (Eph. 4:12). One of the great New Testament teachings is that we are *all* called to ministry.

The eminent twentieth century church renewalist Elton Trueblood made an interesting observation a few years ago when interviewed by the Christian journal *Leadership*:

> I led a retreat in northern Ohio not long ago for twenty-two people, and I went around the circle asking each one to tell what had brought him or her into Christian commitment. I assumed some would mention a public meeting or a sermon. Not one did. They told me about little people, the shoe repairman who made such a testimony in personal living that an impression was created.[2]

If only we could understand that a call to ministry is not reserved for the clergy. What a difference it would make in our lives. Ministry is a resounding theme in Scripture, and it does not begin with ordination, but with commitment and caring.

We each are called to serve, but most of us need encouragement to let go of fears and give more freely. We fear that our
ministry will be boring or unenjoyable, that we may have to do
something embarrassing or something we are ill-prepared for. This
is where I find Abraham's call so helpful.

I am not referring to the traditional interpretation empha-
sizing how much God asked of Abraham: to leave home and
family and set off to lands unknown. Granted, this was a lot to ask,
especially since familial roots meant even more then than they do
today. But God's request was only part of the story. Consider the
rest of the story.

That is to say, consider how much Abraham *wanted* to do
what God had in mind for him. I think of Abraham and picture a
person with an adventurous spirit and wanderlust in his veins.
God *knew* Abraham and called him to a task that suited his unique
personality and skills: "Abraham, I want you to do some traveling
and I want you to father a child." God called on Abraham to *be
himself.*

This is the important insight: As with Abraham, we are not
called to be strangers to ourselves, but to be more fully the person
we were created to be.

What might that entail for you? I heard of a woman whose
pastor preached a sermon on lay ministry and encouraged his
parishioners to find what their call might be. In the midst of
prayer, asking God what she should do, this woman was reminded
of her great smile. The next Sunday she told her pastor, "I found
my ministry. Every Sunday I am going to come early, stay late, and
stand by the door, smiling everyone in and out of the church."

Another woman, unsure of her call, asked her pastor and
heard what most pastors say when they have no suggestions: "Go
home and pray about it." As she did, she began thinking of
students at the nearby university who were away from home, and
she had her plan. She wrote on several three-by-five cards, "Are
you homesick? Come to my house for tea at 4:00 p.m." She posted
the cards around campus, and after a slow start, homesick students
began flocking to her house for tea. When she died ten years later,

eighty pallbearers attended her funeral. All had come to her home for tea and discovered an extraordinary love in the process.

What is your ministry? There is some task, some service tailor-made for everyone. God calls each of us, just like Abraham, to make use of the gifts and strengths we have been given. Ask yourself three questions:

"What tugs at my heart?"
"What do I like to do?"
"What am I good at doing?"

Your call to ministry will likely come out of those three questions. I think of a comment by my former teammate in ministry, Denn Denning:

The church is more than a spiritual outpatient clinic. The church is a training center, with the pastor as the head of the seminary where lay people can be trained theologically and practically and then be sent out as Christian business persons, lawyers, journalists, homemakers, volunteers in the community to be the salt of the earth, the light of the world as Christ's representatives today. We are the ministry to Jesus Christ, alive for God and His Son through the power of the Holy Spirit.[3]

Gifted for Ministry

The most complete biblical treatment of spiritual gifts appears in Paul's letter to the Corinthians:

Now about spiritual gifts, brothers, I do not want you to be ignorant ...

There are different kinds of gifts, but the same Spirit. There are different kinds of service, but the same Lord. There are different kinds of working, but the same God works all of them in all men.

Now to each one the manifestation of the Spirit is given for the common good. To one there is given through the Spirit the message of wisdom, to another the message of knowledge by means of the same Spirit, to another faith by the same Spirit, to another gifts of healing by that one Spirit, to another miraculous powers, to another prophecy, to another distinguishing between spirits, to another speaking in different kinds of tongues, and to still another the interpretation of tongues. All these are the work of one and the same Spirit, and he gives to each one, just as he determines.

The body is a unit, though it is made up of many parts; and though all its parts are many, they form one body. So it is with Christ. For we were all baptized by one Spirit into one body — whether Jews or Greeks, slave or free — and we were all given the one Spirit to drink.

Now the body is not made up of one part but many. If the foot should say, "Because I am not a hand, I do not belong to the body," it would not for that reason cease to be part of the body. And if the ear should say, "Because I am not an eye, I do not belong to the body," it would not for that reason cease to be part of the body.... As it is there are many parts, but one body.

The eye cannot say to the hand, "I don't need you!" And the head cannot say to the feet, "I don't need you!" On the contrary, those parts of the body that seem to be weaker are indispensable. (I Cor. 12:1, 4-16, 20-22, NIV).

Paul makes five statements about spiritual gifts in this letter:

1. There are a variety of gifts.

Paul said, "There are different kinds of gifts," then proceeded to mention some of them: wisdom, knowledge, faith, healing, and miracles. It is important to keep in mind that this is not an exhaustive list, only illustrative. Elsewhere, in Romans 12 and Ephesians 4, he also mentions spiritual gifts, but the list is not the same. In all, twenty-eight different gifts are mentioned in the Bible, but because all the lists give examples and are not exhaustive, there probably are even more. The number is open-ended. New gifts may emerge in every person, in every generation.

2. Every person has at least one spiritual gift.

Paul wrote, "To each one is given the manifestation of the Spirit" (I Cor. 12:7, NIV). This may be one of the most important revelations in Scripture. If ever there was an affirming passage, it is Paul's assurance that each of us has been given a gift by the Holy Spirit. Think again if you are one of those who says, "I'm nothing special. God doesn't have much in mind for me."

I recall something that happened at Christmas time to a clergy colleague of mine. In the spirit and excitement of gift giving, his three-year-old daughter took a big red bow off a package under the tree, placed it on her head, and said, "Look at me, Daddy! I'm a present!"

So are we all — uniquely gifted to help each other.

3. Gifts are to be used.

Paul wrote, "Now to each one the manifestation of the Spirit is given for the common good" (I Cor. 12:7, NIV). The Apostle Peter said something similar: "Each one should use whatever gift he has received to serve others, faithfully administering God's grace in its various forms" (I Peter 4:10, NIV).

At this point a definition is in order. A SPIRITUAL GIFT IS AN UNEARNED, SPECIAL ATTRIBUTE GIVEN BY THE HOLY SPIRIT TO BE USED IN MINISTRY.

In light of Paul's statement and this definition, listen to the words of C. Peter Wagner:

> Every spiritual gift we have is a resource that we must use and for which we will be held responsible at the Judgement. Some will have one, some two, and some five. The quantity does not matter. Stewards are responsible only for what the Master has chosen to give them. But the resource that we do have must be used to accomplish the Master's purpose. There is no time like now to begin to prepare to answer that question which each of us eventually

is going to hear from our Lord: "What did you do with the spiritual gift I gave you?" Tragically, many will not be able to answer that question. They will not be called "good and faithful servants" at least in that area of our lives, because they have been uninformed about spiritual gifts.[4]

4. Gifts are given at the discretion of the Holy Spirit.

Paul wrote, "All these are the work of one and the same Spirit, and he gives them to each one, just as he determines" (I Cor. 12:11, NIV).

Note, the Holy Spirit *gives* the gifts. We cannot create them or take credit for them. Like other things in our lives, they come as gracious gifts from God. Therefore, we are to thank God for them, to use them, but not to boast about them.

5. All gifts are valuable.

Paul affirmed, "The body is a unit though it is made up of many parts; and though all its parts are many they form one body.... The eye cannot say to the hand, 'I don't need you!' And the head cannot say to the feet, 'I don't need you!' On the contrary, those parts of the body that seem to be the weaker are indispensable" (I Cor. 12:12, 21–22, NIV).

In this regard, I recall the time I dislocated a toe playing basketball. I had stolen the ball and was going in for a lay-up, when I was fouled from behind. I hit the floor hard and came up limping. Now, while that toe was functioning normally, I did not pay much attention to it. But after injuring it, I realized how important that miniscule toe was to me. As a result of that injury, I had difficulty walking, let alone playing basketball.

Each of us is gifted in different ways. Some of us are hands. Some of us are eyes. Some of us are knee-caps, but we all serve a valuable purpose in the body. No gift can be ignored. Each gift is indispensable.

Small Groups, Lay Ministry, and Spiritual Gifts

A healthy small group has three primary tasks. The first is to provide a support base, a place where we can be loved, affirmed, and encouraged.

The second task is to help each other discover our unique gifts. We often are blinded to our own special talents. This usually takes one of two forms. We either think too highly of ourselves, like the pastor who insisted he had the gift of preaching, but his congregation did not have the gift of listening! Or, more commonly, we think too little of ourselves. We do not realize how wonderfully gifted we are! To break through this blindness, God calls us into a community of faith where people can get to know us, identify, and call forth our gifts.

I think that is the gist of the "one another" passage from Hebrews:

> And let us consider how we may spur one another on toward love and good deeds. Let us not give up meeting together as some are in the habit of doing, but let us encourage one another. (Hebrews 10:24–25a, NIV)

We can spur one another on by giving encouragement and pointing out how gifted and valuable each of us is. When we begin to recognize and value our own gifts, we are energized. When we experience the joy of knowing why God put us on this earth, what part God wants us to play, we come alive. We are spurred on to greater things.

The third task of a healthy, small group is to hold each other accountable for using our gifts in ministry. Remember Jesus' model? "He appointed twelve — designating them apostles — that they might be with him and that he might send them out to preach" (Mark 3:14, NIV). We need to follow that model of coming together (fellowship) and going out (ministry).

David Hubbard, president of Fuller Theological Seminary, speaks clearly of the need for "one anothering" in ministry:

Christians sometimes make a severe mistake . . . Because we believe that Christ is sufficient for all our needs, we think that we should not need other people. What we don't realize is that one of Christ's most effective ways of caring for us is other people he brings into our lives. God, from the beginning, never intended human beings to live alone. Family and friends have been part of His program for our good from the start.

Jesus himself spent his early life in the warmth of a family, and his mature years in the fellowship of friends. Peter, James, John, Mary, Martha, and Lazarus were among those friendships Jesus treasured.

The Apostle Paul surrounded himself with friends and fellow workers. Courage he had plenty of. Shipwreck, imprisonment, torture were not strangers to him. He stood before king and emperor and declared his faith with boldness. Yet, he was dependent on his friends. He needed other people. He almost always traveled with friends like Barnabas, Silas, and Timothy. And his letters — particularly those like Colossians, written at the end of his life — attest the breadth and depth of his friendships. To his friends Paul looked for support through prayer, concern for his welfare, and partnership in mission.[5]

Paul depended upon his friends to spur him on. So do I. There have been many a Tuesday evening when I have been tempted to skip my small group. I had a busy day. I was tired. I just wanted to stay at home, put my feet up, and watch TV or read a book. But I went to the group and, almost invariably, I was glad I did. Just being with those friends, as they prayed for me and supported me, lifted my spirit, both physically and emotionally. In fact, I have noticed that the times I am tempted to miss the group are the times I get the most out of the group! After a group meeting, I am ready to face another day with renewed hope and energy.

My small group regularly spurs me on to greater things. I bet your group does the same for you!

STUDY TEN:
Spurring One Another on Toward Love and Good Deeds

1. **Check-In** *(15–20 minutes)*

    - What was a gift you received that you will long remember?
    - What was something you enjoyed doing today?

2. **Exploration** *(50–60 minutes)*

    Spend fifteen or twenty minutes discussing the chapter. What challenged you? What upset you? What comforted you?

    Then use the remaining time (35–40 minutes) to complete this "Identifying Gifts" exercise.

    Each person needs a set of three-by-five cards, one card for every member of the group, excluding him- or herself. (If ten people are present, everyone should have nine cards. If six are present, everyone should have five cards.) At the top of each card, write the name of a group member. Then look over the list below of the twenty-eight gifts mentioned in Scripture, plus "Other," which you may think of.

    For each person, select one or two gifts that fit for them, and write the gifts down on a card, along with a short statement for that person. For instance, one card might read: "WALT — EXHORTATION — I SEE YOU CONTINUALLY AFFIRMING THE BEST IN PEOPLE." After all cards are completed, give them to the people named. Each person reads over the cards, silently reflecting for three to five minutes upon the gifts identified for him or her. Then each takes a couple of minutes sharing their responses to the cards — either accepting, rejecting, or questioning any gifts mentioned.

SPIRITUAL GIFTS MENTIONED IN SCRIPTURE

Prophecy	Service	Teaching
Exhortation	Giving	Leadership
Mercy	Wisdom	Knowledge
Faith	Healing	Miracles
Tongues	Discernment	Interpretation of Tongues
Apostle	Helps	Administration
Evangelism	Pastor	Celibacy
Martyrdom	Hospitality	Voluntary Poverty
Missionary	Intercession	Exorcism
Craftsmanship	Other: _____	

3. **Prayer Concerns** *(20–30 minutes)*

4. **Prayer** *(5–10 minutes)*

5. **Assignment**
   Assign Chapter 11 for next week's reading.

"Dear Timothy, I'm sending under separate cover extra copies of the spiritual gifts inventory quiz for your church."

© 1986 Erik Johnson

CHAPTER 11

Release **O**NE **A**nother

or Covenant with

Another **O**NE

*On that day
the Lord made a new convenant
with Abram.*

Genesis 15:18 (NIV)

This final chapter addresses the question, "Do you want your small group to continue or to end?" We have investigated eight key "one another" building blocks for small groups. We have looked at:

Loving one another
Praying for one another
Caring for one another
Bearing one another's burdens
Encouraging one another
Submitting to one another
Admonishing one another
Spurring one another on toward love and good deeds

We have seen how these "one another" passages instruct us in relating to one another within the Body of Christ, and we have determined how they directly concern small group life. Now it is time to decide what is next, whether it is time to continue or to end your small group.

Whichever your group decides, it is important to set aside time to talk about it. This is an important crossroad in small group life, for how your group makes the decision will affect your willingness to be part of a small group in the future. If the ending is not handled properly, you may hesitate before joining another small group. The same goes for continuing the group. If your group does not adequately discuss how you want to proceed, unnecessary future problems may arise. It is important to be clear about future group ground rules. The decisions your group makes at this point are crucial. In the language of small group dynamics, you are facing the critical issues of CLOSURE or CONTRACTING.

Closure

The lifespan of a typical small group is about two years, though I have been part of one meeting weekly for twelve. Still others may go from three weeks to little over a year. However long a group lasts, closure with one another is extremely important when the group decides to end its life together or when an individual member decides to leave. There are three reasons.

Number one has to do with saying good-byes. I dislike good-byes; they are difficult to say. I dislike facing the fact that relationships with people will change. We no longer will spend the same kind of time together. We may continue seeing one another, but it will not be the same. Significant relationships and friendships require constant maintenance. When a person leaves a group or the group disbands, relationships fall into disrepair unless we make time to see those people in some way on a regular basis — and that is not likely to happen.

I think of the time a good friend of mine Dave Hosick moved miles away from me to Pennsylvania. Dave and I had been in a weekly clergy group for four years. "Well," he said, when he left, "this is probably the last time we'll ever see each other again. We'll be miles apart and, unless we stumble across one another at denominational gatherings, this could be it for us."

My immediate response was, "You sure are pessimistic!" But I have come to appreciate his realism, for the truth is we have not seen each other since. And if we downplay our good-byes — gloss over them by saying, "Oh, we'll see each other again," or "Nothing will change between us; we will still see each other at church" — we are likely fooling ourselves. Not facing the reality and even the pain of good-byes can leave us in a world of hurt. We carry an unfinished relationship in our bodies.

I still remember vividly my bumbled good-bye to Hank. It took place at Coco's restaurant, where we had met for lunch every Monday for five years. He was (and still is) a friend, confidant, and cheerleader in my life. At the time, I was moving from Omaha, Nebraska, to Brookings, Oregon, and it was to be our last lunch together. Unfortunately, I ate lunch without telling him how much he had meant to me and how I valued our friendship. Perhaps I was afraid to face the change 1,500 miles would bring to our relationship. After arriving in Oregon, I realized how many "thank-yous" and sentiments for Hank I had left unsaid. I later communicated those sentiments via cassette tape, but I had missed the joy of saying them face-to-face.

That experience taught me, albeit the hard way, that one of the greatest gifts we can give one another is setting aside time to say good-bye. It brings us current to the moment of parting and keeps us from carrying around a load of unsaid feelings.

The second reason for group closure has to do with review. It is important to set aside time in which we can review the experiences we shared together, both good and bad.

There is a touching scene in the children's book *Charlotte's Web* where Charlotte, a spider, has just saved the life of a pig named Wilbur. But now Charlotte is near death and they have the following conversation:

> "Charlotte, why did you do this for me? I don't deserve it. I've never done anything for you."
>
> "You have been my friend," replied Charlotte. "That in itself is a tremendous thing."
>
> "Well," said Wilbur, "I'm no good at making speeches. I haven't got your gift for words. But you saved me, Charlotte, and I would gladly give my life for you — I really would."
>
> Charlotte replied, "I'm sure you would. And I thank you for your generous sentiments." [1]

Tragically, we let people slip away without telling them what they have meant to us. Setting aside time for closure honors the time we have spent together and provides an opportunity to say what we enjoyed about one another, as well as what was good and what was bad for us in the group.

The third reason for closure has to do with clarity. When we set aside time for closure, we know *why* individuals are leaving and/or why the group will no longer be meeting.

Two instances come to mind. One has to do with a couple formerly in our small group. They stayed with us for a year, then abruptly stopped attending without a word as to why. I still wonder. Did we do something to offend them? Were they looking for something else in a small group? What was it? We will never know. They may have wanted to spare us the pain of being confronted over insensitive behavior on our part. However, if so, they left us with a lot of questions and pain nonetheless. We would have much preferred knowing, instead of wondering.

The other instance involved a small group that had been meeting together for a year. They took the summer off, planning to reconvene in the fall. When October moved into November, however, they still had not met. In fact, they never would again. Their group simply dissolved. One of the members tried to get the group together once more, to say good-bye and celebrate the time they had shared together, but everyone was too busy. "Let's just leave it as it is," they said. Hurt and disappointed, the member who tried to have them meet and say their good-byes was reluctant to join another small group. She wondered if she had done something wrong and, when asked if she wanted to join another group, she said, "I need to wait for a while. My last group and the way we left things has left a bad taste in my mouth."

Not facing the good-bye, not saying what needs to be said in terms of closure, leaves an ugly residue that is hard to wipe off. If you are thinking of leaving the group, take time to say good-bye. Mention what was good about the group. Talk about what you gained from it. Also, share how the group might have been better for you and why you have decided to leave. Such open and honest sharing will be better for you and the group in the long run.

Contracting

If your group is discussing and deciding to continue on, the next steps you take are just as important as those for closure. It is imperative to have a clear group contract (or group covenant) under which to operate.

A contract is an agreed-upon understanding of group rules, guidelines, and disciplines. Whether or not it is formally recognized, a contract actually exists already when you have a small group. It may be assumed and never articulated or written down, but your continued participation indicates some level of agreement.

However, the most helpful type of contract for a small group is one that is discussed, negotiated, and recorded. Studies in

small group dynamics reveal that people are more highly committed to groups in which they have had some say about its direction
and functioning. Moreover, a negotiated contract, recorded on
paper, gives the group more identity and direction, while lessening
the risk of future misunderstanding. It helps focus members'
hopes, needs, and desires; and it is a ready, clear, and specific
record of the decisions made in case questions arise about group
norms and guidelines. A written, negotiated contract also provides
a solid base for future group evaluations. If a group continues
meeting for many months or years, it will not have to recreate the
wheel during regular evaluation times, only fine-tune the existing
contract. (Speaking of evaluation times — an ongoing small group
should evaluate its life together every three or four months to
build in a gracious time for some members to leave, as well as
provide a regular fine-tuning process for the group).

Points to consider in a small group contract include:

PURPOSE
- Why do we want to have this group?
- What do we hope to get out of it?
- What will make the group "successful"?

DURATION
- How long will we meet before evaluating the group once again?
- How long are we willing to commit to this group? Six weeks?
  Twelve weeks? Four months? A year? More?

TIME
- How often (weekly, twice a month, monthly) and for how long
  (one hour, two hours, all day) will the group meet? Generally
  speaking, the more often and longer a group meets, the deeper
  the sharing and commitment members feel. For example, a
  group that meets weekly for two hours will likely form deeper
  relationships than the group that meets every other Thursday
  over lunch, all other things being equal.

- How will the time be divided? A common pattern for a weekly, two-hour evening group might be:
    - 30 minutes – Check-In
    - 45 minutes – Study
    - 30 minutes – Sharing prayer requests
    - 15 minutes – Prayer

  A noon-hour group might adopt the following:
    - 12:00–12:10 – Check-In
    - 12:10–12:25 – Study
    - 12:25–12:45 – Share
    - 12:45–12:50 – Pray
- Who will keep time during the group?
- Are we committed to beginning and ending on time?

PLACE
- Will the group meet in homes or offices, at a restaurant or the church?
- Will we meet in the same place every time or rotate meeting places?

LEADERSHIP
- Who will enable the group?
- Will we rotate leadership, with everyone taking turns?
- Will we choose one designated leader who will lead us for the duration of this contract?
- Will only two or three take turns?

PARTICIPATION
- Who is this group for? Couples? Singles? Intergenerational? Mixed?
- Is the group "open" (new people can drop in any time) or "closed" (we will not accept new members until the contract is up)?

ATTENDANCE
- What priority are we willing to give to the group?

- What is a valid excuse for not coming?
- Do we call everyone in the group when we cannot be present or only the host/hostess or leader? Something to consider: Unless there is a core of people who commit to coming regularly, the group will not last very long.

EXITING
- Will we agree not to leave the group without having a time of closure?
- Are we willing to stay in the group until the next evaluation period?

EVALUATION
- How often will we evaluate the group? Quarterly? Monthly? Twice a year?
- How will we do the evaluation?
- Will we do it ourselves or call in outside help?
- How much time will we set aside to do this?

STUDY
- What do we want to study next? The Bible? Tapes? A book?
- How will we decide?

MINISTRY
- Will we have a task or mission?
- Will we be open to a ministry at some later date?
- Will this be as a group or as individuals supported by the group?

REFRESHMENTS
- Refreshments can help or hinder the life of the group. Will we have them?
- If so, how elaborate? Self-serve?
- When during the meeting will we have them? At the beginning, in the middle, at the end of the group meeting?

CHILDREN
- Are children to be present?
- If meeting in a home with children, will a babysitter be necessary?

PERSONAL DISCIPLINES
- Will I pray for each person daily?
- Will I read the assigned reading for the group?
- Will I keep all confidences within the group?

If your group decides to continue, a sample group contract is provided at the end of the chapter. Remember that we are a covenanting (contracting) people. God made a covenant with Noah, Abraham, and Moses. God promised a new covenant to Jeremiah, and Jesus became the mediator of that covenant. So, following God's lead, we covenant or contract with one another.

We also contract with one another for preventative maintenance reasons. As the saying goes, "An ounce of prevention is worth a pound of cure." Unfortunately, many needless group problems arise due to an unclear group contract. Those problems can be avoided, however, if you take time now to write a clear contract for your group.

May God bless you and your group beyond your wildest expectations as you share your lives with one another!

STUDY ELEVEN
Closure or Contract

1. **Check-In** *(20–30 minutes)*
   Complete these sentences:

   - "If I could re-live part of my week because it was so good, I would re-live ..."
   - "If I could re-do part of my past week because it was so bad, I would ..."

2. **Next Steps** *(40–50 minutes)*

   a. Begin by sharing three things you enjoyed about these studies and/or this small group experience. What are a couple of things you would like to have done differently or would like to see changed in the group?
   b. Discuss whether or not the group will continue.
   c. *If the entire group decides to disband,* share what the group meant to you, what you learned from it, and what you will miss by not being together any longer. After the open time of sharing is complete, share prayer requests and close in prayer, thanking God for the gifts you have received from the experience of being in a group.
   d. *If some members of the group decide to continue on,* move next to sharing whether or not you want to stay in the group and some of the reasons for your decision.

      If some members decide to leave the group, allow time to say good-bye. Ask those who are leaving what they will miss about the group. In addition, share important memories about their involvement in the group and what they will miss about no longer being there.

      From here move into prayer requests and prayer (below), leaving the formation of a group contract until the next time you meet. As the group closes in prayer, have the individuals who are leaving sit in the middle of a circle, lay hands on them and pray for them in the next chapter of their lives. Take time to say good-bye.

      If no one decides to leave the group, move right into contracting. Fill out the Group Contract at the end of this chapter. Base your discussion of the contract on the "Points to consider" section of this chapter.

3. **Prayer Concerns** *(20–30 minutes)*

4. **Prayer** *(10 minutes)*

GROUP COVENANT

Our group goals are: _____

_____

_____

_____

What we intend to study is: _____

We have covenanted together to meet for _____ weeks, at which time we will review and evaluate our group.

We will meet each week on _____. We will begin at _____ and close at _____.   (day of week)
(time)   (time)

A typical schedule will look like: _____

_____

_____

Ground Rules:

Food: _____   Dress: _____

Children: _____   Place: _____

Absence: _____   Leadership
Responsibility: _____

Individual Preparation and
Responsibility: _____   Visitors: _____

Evaluation
Procedures: _____   Re-evaluation
Time: _____

_____   Open (e.g., new people can come
any time) or Closed Group (e.g.,
after 3rd meeting, no new members):

Telephone
Interruptions: _____   _____

Decision Making: _____   Ministry (group or support
individual): _____

Personal Disciplines: _____

I will try, with God's help, to be a regular, faithful, involved, caring member of this Covenant Group.

Signed _____

Notes

Chapter 1
1. Edward Bauman, THE BIBLE AND NEW LIFE FOR THE CHURCH (Arlington, VA: Bauman Bible Telecasts, Inc., 1976), 39.
2. Alan Loy McGinnis, BRINGING OUT THE BEST IN PEOPLE (Minneapolis: Augsburg Fortress Publishers, 1985), 40.
3. The books I was reading included: *Joining Together: Group Theory and Group Skills*, by David Johnson and Frank Johnson; *Cultivating Religious Growth Groups*, by Charles Olsen; *Groups that Work*, by Walden Howard; *Small Group Communication: A Reader*, by Robert Cathcart and Larry Samovar; *Getting Together*, by Em Griffen; and *Using the Bible in Groups*, by Roberta Hestenes.

Chapter 2
1. Taken from a television interview with Will Durant.
2. Leon Morris, TESTAMENTS OF LOVE: A STUDY OF LOVE IN THE BIBLE (Grand Rapids, MI: William B. Eerdmans Publishing Company).
3. John Killinger, A DEVOTIONAL GUIDE TO JOHN (Irving, TX: Word Inc., 1981), 98.
4. William Barclay, THE GOSPEL OF JOHN, VOL. 2 (from *The Daily Study Bible Series*) (Louisville, KY: Westminster/John Knox Press, 1956).
5. Alan Loy McGinnis, THE FRIENDSHIP FACTOR (Minneapolis: Augsburg Fortress Publishers, 1979), 51.
6. Louis Evans, Jr., COVENANT TO CARE (formerly CREATIVE LOVE) (Wheaton, IL: Victor Books, 1989), 45.
7. Bruce Larson, "None of Us Are Sinners Emeritus," LEADERSHIP, Fall 1984, 13–14.
8. Roberta Hestenes, USING THE BIBLE IN GROUPS (Louisville, KY: Westminster/John Knox Press, 1983), 28.
9. David Redding, JESUS MAKES ME LAUGH (Grand Rapids, MI: Zondervan Publishing House, 1977), 36.

Chapter 3
1. Ben Patterson, "The Central Work of Prayer," LEADERSHIP, Winter 1982, 114.
2. Ibid., 114.
3. Louis Evans, Jr., COVENANT TO CARE (formerly CREATIVE LOVE) (Wheaton, IL: Victor Books, 1989), 55.

Chapter 4
1. Russell P. Spittler, THE CORINTHIAN CORRESPONDENCE (Springfield, MO: The Gospel Publishing House, 1976), 7.
2. WEBSTER'S NEW WORLD DICTIONARY (New York: Simon & Schuster, 1988).
3. M. Scott Peck, THE ROAD LESS TRAVELED (New York: Simon & Schuster, 1978), 120–21.
4. Morton Kelsey, CARING (Ramsey, NJ: Paulist Press, 1981), 67.
5. Paul Tournier, TO UNDERSTAND EACH OTHER (Louisville, KY: Westminster/John Knox Press, 1967), 8.
6. Quote from George Parson's "Conflict Management Through Small Groups," conference tape, The Alban Institute.
7. Mother Theresa quote which appeared in Malcolm Muggeridge's SOMETHING BEAUTIFUL FOR GOD (New York: Harper & Row, Publishers, Inc., 1971).

Chapter 5
1. Maxie Dunham, CCNT: VOL 8 COMMUNICATOR'S COMMENTARY (Irving, TX: Word, Inc., 1982), 122.
2. Charles R. Swindoll, GROWING STRONG IN THE SEASONS OF LIFE (Portland, OR: Multnomah Press, 1983), 365.
3. "What a Friend We Have in Jesus," words by Joseph M. Scriven, ca. 1855.
4. Quoted by Paul D. Robbins in "Must Men Be Friendless," LEADERSHIP, Fall 1984, 26.
5. John Powell, WHY AM I AFRAID TO TELL YOU WHO I AM? (Chicago: Peacock Books, Part of Argus Communications, 1969).
6. Vance Havner, from a quotation in LEADERSHIP, Winter 1983, 94.
7. Ken Medema, from his song "If This Is Not The Place," published by Word Music, 1977.

Chapter 6
1. Benjamin Franklin quote from THE BEST OF THE COCKLE BUR, compiled and edited by Harry B. Otis. (Omaha, NE: The Bur Inc., 1987), 185.
2. William Barclay, THE LETTERS OF JAMES AND PETER (from *The Daily Study Bible Series*) (Louisville, KY: Westminster/John Knox Press, 1960), 100.
3. Louis Evans, Jr., COVENANT TO CARE (formerly CREATIVE LOVE) (Wheaton, IL: Victor Books, 1989), 92.

Chapter 7
1. Bruce Larson and Keith Miller, THE PASSIONATE PEOPLE (Waco, TX: Word Books, 1979).
2. Charles R. Swindoll, THE QUEST FOR CHARACTER (Portland, OR: Multnomah Press, 1983).
3. Fulton J. Sheen, THE WIT & WISDOM OF BISHOP FULTON J. SHEEN, edited by Bill Adler (New York: Simon & Schuster, Doubleday Edition, Prentice Hall, Inc., 1968), 153.
4. Wes Seeliger, "Froghood," FAITH AT WORK MAGAZINE, February 1972, 13.
5. Lyman Coleman, BEGINNINGS: SIX LESSONS TO BECOME A SUPPORT GROUP, (Littleton, CO: Serendipity House, Inc., 1987), 20–21.

Chapter 8
1. James Dobson, STRAIGHT TALK TO MEN AND THEIR WIVES (Irving, TX: Word, Inc., 1980), 58–60.
2. Philip Crosby, THE ART OF GETTING YOUR OWN SWEET WAY, Second Edition (New York: McGraw-Hill, Inc., 1982).
3. William Barclay, THE ACTS OF THE APOSTLES (from *The Daily Study Bible Series*) (Louisville, KY: Westminster/John Knox Press, 1955), 170.
4. Richard Foster, CELEBRATION OF DISCIPLINE (New York: Harper & Row, Publishers, Inc., 1978), 97.
5. Louis Evans, Jr., COVENANT TO CARE (formerly CREATIVE LOVE) (Wheaton, IL: Victor Books, 1989), 103.
6. Lloyd John Ogilvie, GOD'S BEST FOR MY LIFE (Eugene, OR: Harvest House Publishers, 1981), 123.

Chapter 9
1. WEBSTER'S NEW WORLD DICTIONARY (New York: Simon & Schuster, 1989).
2. M. Scott Peck, THE DIFFERENT DRUM (New York: Simon & Schuster, 1987), 62–64.
3. Martin Bolt and David Myers, THE HUMAN CONNECTION (Downers Grove, IL: InterVarsity Press, 1984), 99.
4. Morton Kelsey, CARING (Ramsey, NJ: Paulist Press, 1981), 25–26.
5. David Augsburger, CARING ENOUGH TO CONFRONT (Glendale, CA: Regal Books, 1978).
6. Ralph Osborne, "Ideas for Groups," FAITH AT WORK MAGAZINE, February 1976, 19.

Chapter 10
1. Robert Slocum, MAXIMUM MINISTRY (Colorado Springs: Nav Press, 1990).
2. Elton Trueblood, "A Time for Holy Dissatisfaction," LEADERSHIP, Winter 1983, 21–22.
3. From a sermon by Denn Denning, "A Contagious Laity," preached at the San Marino Community Church, San Marino, CA, January 9, 1983.
4. C. Peter Wagner, YOUR SPIRITUAL GIFTS CAN HELP YOUR CHURCH GROW (Ventura, CA: Regal Books, a division of Gospel Light Publications, 1980), 55.
5. David Allen Hubbard, COLOSSIANS SPEAKS TO THE SICKNESS OF OUR TIMES (Irving, TX: Word Publishing, 1976), 88–89.

Chapter 11
1. E.B. White, CHARLOTTE'S WEB (New York: Harper & Row, Publishers, Inc., 1952), 164–65.

RICHARD C. MEYER served the church in pastoral ministry for 25 years. He has pastored small (250 members), medium (800 members), and large (1275 members) congregations in the Presbyterian church. In the fall of 2000, he left pastoral ministry to follow his passion of calling people into deep spiritual community through small groups. He currently is devoting his energies to the formation of The One Anothering Institute, a consulting resource for churches.

Meyer is a much sought-after conference speaker and small group consultant, chairperson of the Faith at Work Board, and a regular columnist for the *Faith @ Work Magazine*. His *One Anothering* series, of which this third volume is the culmination, has been called "the best book on church groups I have ever seen!"